*"Let all the ends thou aim'st at be thy country's,
thy God's, and truth's."*
— Shakespeare's *Henry VIII*

Politicians signing the *Fair Campaign Practice Act* (UPI photo).

HONEST GOVERNMENT

CHARLES S. NORBURN, M.D.

New Puritan Library

Illustrated bar graphs by Richard F. Brooks

Copyright © 1984 by Charles S. Norburn, M.D.

P.O. Box 5216
Asheville, North Carolina 28813

All rights reserved. Permission for reprinted portions or other editions must be sought in writing from New Puritan Library, Inc., 91 Lytle Road, Fletcher, NC 28732. Short excerpts, up to three paragraphs for review purposes, are hereby permitted.

Library of Congress Number: 84-060275
ISBN 0-932050-25-5

Addresses of publications which are prime sources for material in *Honest Government:*

Acres, USA (article on seed monopolies)
Box 9547, Raytown, MO 64133

Don Bell Reports (list of corporation interlocks)
P.O. Box 2223, Palm Beach, FL 33480

Spotlight
300 Independence Ave. S.E., Washington, DC 20003

U.S. News & World Report
2400 N. Street, Washington, DC 20037

United Press International (3 photos)
220 East 42nd Street, New York, NY 10017

Contents

Chapter 1: The Constitutional Selection of
           Federal Officials and the Change 1

Chapter 2: Presidential Elections 15

Chapter 3: Congressional Elections 41

Chapter 4: Charters, Corporations and Mergers 53

Chapter 5: Monopoly on Food 59

Chapter 6: The Giveaway of Our
           Natural Resources 77

Chapter 7: Utilities 99

Chapter 8: The Pentagon 105

Chapter 9: The Arch-Criminals 109

Chapter 10: The Nation's Monetary System 115

Chapter 11: Taxes 119

Chapter 12:	Corporate Taxes 131
Chapter 13:	Foundations 135
Chapter 14:	"Free Trade" or National Suicide? ... 139
Chapter 15:	Boring From Within 145
Chapter 16:	Internationalism 151
Chapter 17:	The Dregs of Exploitation 169
Chapter 18:	The Dreary Life of Debt 173
Chapter 19:	Federal Intrusion 183
Chapter 20:	A Glance Backward and a Look Ahead 189
Chapter 21:	Regaining Our Government: A Return to the *U.S. Constitution* 195

THE APPENDIX

Appendix A:	*The Mayflower Compact:* 1620 211
Appendix B:	*The Declaration of Independence:* 1776 213
Appendix C:	*The Constitution of the United States of America:* 1789 ... 219
Index:	 247

CHAPTER 1

The Constitutional Selection of Federal Officials and the Change

The new world that became the United States of America was a veritable paradise, filled with beauty and natural resources, and the *Constitution* for the new nation was the best ever devised. There was to be no class system. This government was to be small, quiet, unobtrusive — a friend to the people it served. Its function was to protect every law-abiding citizen alike. It was to protect him in his God-given right to life, freedom to come and go, freedom of thought, of religion, and of association, freedom to use his own efforts in the development of his natural talents and capabilities, and to choose his own occupation. The government provided for a system of private and corporate capitalism and free enterprise — the right of every citizen to earn property and to hold it. We have strayed far from that ideal beginning.

To the casual observer all seems serene and prosperous. Streets are filled with cars, stores with shoppers; there are great throngs of people at sporting events. Analysts report that the recession has passed, that this is still the richest nation in the world.

We look at these things and tend to turn away from the dimmer picture — the one that forecasts our future.

Human greed, the thirst for power, changed our *Constitution*. Since then the necessity of federal officials to sell their souls for office has diverted our government from its rightful course, and made it unworthy of a great people. If this corruption is allowed to continue, enormously wealthy men will take over all property. There will be the loss of our nation's independence, and at the last, some form of dictatorship will come, with death for millions of our people and economic slavery for others.

This need not continue. We can put a stop to it. The citizens of this nation, laying all thought of self aside, can reclaim our government. Needed is a thorough understanding of the problem, our danger, the necessity for action, and the direction this action should take.

Let us start at the beginning and advance step by step to our present condition. Let us see how all this came about, and then read on for a glance at the true state of the union. This will not only give the reader a realization of the necessity for prompt action; it will give a clearer understanding for the book's recommendations.

Early Selection of Federal Officials

The writers of the *Constitution,* with their system of checks and balances, wanted to insure a stable government, steadfast in purpose, beyond the demands of special interests and vagaries of the people. Thus it was necessary that a part of the government be placed beyond the direct control of the people governed. The executive branch, the Presidency, and one branch of the Legislature, the Senate, were set aside. These officials were to be entirely free from personal political ambitions and obligations. They were to be free from today's ever-present awareness of the need to appeal to wealthy men for campaign money, and appeal to various minorities for votes. It was realized also that the people, taken as a whole, could not know and select the nation's or states' best men for these high offices. Legislators of the states, elected and answerable to the people, better able to choose, were charged with this important responsibility. For selection of the President and Vice President the legislators of each state selected some of the states' ablest men as members of an Electoral College, in number as many as that state has senators and representatives in Washington. The duty of this College was to consider every outstanding man of the nation, and from these to choose the President and Vice President. Any tie was to be broken by the United States House of Representatives.

Under this system great men who might not have sought office were drawn into service of their country. Washington, John Adams, Jefferson, Madison, Monroe and John Quincey Adams were selected this way.

Each state Legislature chose and appointed its two senators from the state's greatest men. All the states were to be represented equally in the Senate, thus preventing populous states, with perhaps large ethnic or other close groups, from seeking special consideration and dominating the Senate.

Then came the direct voice of the people in their federal government. Congressional districts were relatively small. Those who wrote the *Constitution* must have presumed that candidates for the office of U.S. representatives could be known by the people; thus the *Constitution* provided that these officials were to be chosen by direct vote of the people. These representatives were the only federal officials to be placed at the direct beck and call of their constituents.

Although the people directly controlled only one-half of

the legislative branch of the federal government, their voice was very great. Their representatives held veto power over all legislation, as did the President and the Senate. The House of Representatives stood first in assessing federal taxes.

The rest of the *Constitution* is mainly devoted to statements of powers and duties. One of these is of especial interest here. It refers to the issue and control of the new nation's money. The Revolutionary War was not fought over a tax on tea or any such trifle. The war was fought because the wealthy men who owned the Bank of England, acting through Parliament and the King, were determined to control the Colonists' money. The Colonists were just as determined that they, themselves, should control their medium of exchange. Time and time again the Colonists had issued their own money, only to have it suppressed by the English overlords. This conflict finally reached the boiling point.

After years of struggle and privation, after the sacrifice of great treasure and many lives, the Colonists won. In their *Constitution,* Section 8, Paragraph 5, Congress is given power "To coin money, regulate the value thereof and of foreign coin."

This provision of government control of its money, and a private capitalistic system of free enterprise, were the very foundations of our nation. By definition the goods upon the shelves of a little grocery store (its eggs, sacks of flour, and canned goods), the horse and plow of a little farmer as he raises vegetables for sale, are *capital,* as well as a billionaire's factory. Capitalism, private and corporate, is the foundation of our economy. Its proper use in free enterprise is laid down in the definition of this term in *Webster's Dictionary:* "freedom of private business to organize and operate for profit within a competitive system, without interference by government beyond regulations necessary to protect public interest and keep the national economy in balance."

Everything here seemed settled forever. Never was there a purer, more ideal vision of government. If the *Constitution,* as written, had been followed, and the government had issued and controlled its own money, used it as necessary and needed, and loaned it at interest, there would be, even now, no national debt and little federal taxes. If this and a true system of free enterprise had been adhered to, the light from this nation would have shone throughout the world, attracting other converts. With such an example there would have been no place for socialism or communism. Most of the enormous waste of armament would have been avoided, and most of the destructive wars would not have been fought. What went wrong?

As seen now, the *Constitution,* itself, the noblest document of fundamental laws ever penned, suffered from serious omissions. There should have been a provision that in the election of U.S. representatives, each Congressional district should be an island — that no person or corporation residing outside the district could send aid or come in to interfere. There should also have been a provision that the only campaign money a candidate could receive would be small limited amounts contributed in passing the hat at political rallies. Further, public officials should have been forbidden from accepting monetary or any other valuable favors, including later employment, from those who might have a personal financial interest in their official actions. The penalty for this should be a heavy fine and imprisonment for both giver and taker of a bribe.

The reason for such omissions is easily understood. Most of those who signed the *Constitution* were patriotic men of high character. It could not have occurred to them that some men love themselves more than they love their country. They could not envision a time when bribing public servants, and official handing out of special privileges or the nation's property, would be the order of the day. There were such men representing special interests even then. They were the same men and the same type of men who owned the Bank of England. One of these was among the signers.

Alexander Hamilton, banker, headed the delegation from New York. Before the signing he tried to have the nation's money given to bankers. When this was refused, he quit the convention.

The convention marked time. Hamilton returned. He had a plan. The *Constitution* was adopted. Hamilton secured the office of Secretary of the Treasury. He at once introduced in the House of Representatives a report providing that the nation's money be controlled by bankers. Thomas Jefferson and others sounded the warning, but their voices were drowned out. The tactics of such wealthy bankers are well known. They have been repeated thousands of times. Politics, domination and greed are their business. By demand, insistence, perseverance, ridicule of opposition, molding of public opinion through their newspapers, and bribery of public officials, they get their way.

Bankers took over the new nation's monetary system. They established the misnamed United States Bank in December, 1791. This bank was largely financed by the government. It printed paper money and loaned it at interest, for private profit, just as the English bankers had done. Thus, in this most important aspect, the Revolutionary War had been fought in vain.

Yet, even this was not enough for these wealthy men. Our system of electing federal officials was too idealistic, too restrictive for those whose personal interest came before the national interest — for those who wanted control of the government as a means of obtaining the nation's natural resources, and expanding their personal power and fortune. Under the pretense of giving the people the vote and more power, all power was taken from them. The change destroyed the independent judgment of federal officials, and single-minded loyalty in the service of their country.

Andrew Jackson, a war hero, was selected for the Presidency. He knew that he would not be selected again. He introduced the popular vote for the Presidency in 1832. The spoils system became an increasing part of the federal government.

Political bosses of each major political party, in agreement with financiers, named Presidential and Vice Presidential candidates of each party. The financiers paid most of the campaign expenses of both and left the choice to the voters. (The two-party system was not envisioned by the signers of the *Constitution*.)

Abraham Lincoln came like a breath of fresh air. He was elected in a three-way race by a plurality of under 40 percent. After him there was mediocrity and corruption.

The evils of private control of the nation's money and of private influence in government were cumulative. President Grant was inaugurated in 1869. That was the year the last spike was driven in the first transcontinental railroad. Millions of acres of priceless land with its timber and minerals were given to those who built the railroads — not just rights of way, but everywhere. Mount Saint Helens was given. Corruption in government reached a new high. Del Mar tells the story of intrigue and treachery. From the history of the following years, it seems that any bill the financiers wanted was passed by Congress. Any property of the nation which they coveted was given. A number of today's great fortunes were founded on those gifts.

The first drive by financiers to take over the nation itself came during President Woodrow Wilson's disastrous terms in office. Great banks such as Kuhn-Loeb, an American branch of Rothschild's European banks, gave much of the money for Wilson's campaign expenses. The bankers placed Colonel Edward M. House at Wilson's side — to direct the course of government.

On February 25, 1913, the *Constitution* was amended to introduce the income tax. On May 31, 1913, the *Constitution* was ratified to elect U.S. senators by popular vote. And on December 23, 1913, the *Constitution* was overruled and the Federal Reserve Act became law. The Federal Reserve Act allowed financiers, controlling the system, to create money by a line in a ledger, receive U.S. bonds for it, and on these bonds receive interest from the government, and in their private banks lend the money at interest.

In his second term in office, elected upon a peace platform, President Wilson led America into World War I to protect bankers' loans abroad.

The stage was set for the immediate takeover of the nation. There was a drive made to surrender our independence to a League of Nations, controlled by those who promoted world government. Although this attempt failed, these wealthy men never gave up.

The Great Depression

The Federal Reserve's outpouring of money in the early twenties, followed by an almost total shutting off of money, caused the great depression of the 1930's.

Then bankers engineered the taking of the people's gold by putting it in Fort Knox where they could raid it. By withholding money from those who owed it to them, they broke thousands of small businesses, thus increasing their monopoly.

The bankers added amendment after amendment to the Federal Reserve Act, increasing their hold on the nation's economy. Details on all these matters are given in my earlier book, *Honest Money.*

President Franklin D. Roosevelt did not correct the root cause of the depression by repealing the Federal Reserve Act of 1913, in order to place the issue and control of money with Congress, as the *Constitution* dictates. He let that evil stand, and started another one: welfare for the Federal Reserve's victims, which made millions dependent on the government for their economic survival.

Once the government became the provider, the floodgates were open. Those people placed on welfare could vote; obviously, they voted for those who gave them the most benefits. Soon, acquiring a taste of getting something for nothing, they began to raise their demands for more and more. The politicians gave them food stamps, money for fatherless children and their mothers, student loans, housing, loans to farmers and businesses. The cost of social programs has now become the largest item of the national budget, larger than the defense budget. Reaching hundreds of billions of dollars a year, this bill must be paid by the taxpayers who can least afford it, or by the Federal Reserve increasing the federal debt. From all this it was but a step to "affirmative action." Males who should be the breadwinners of their families are discriminated against and denied employment. Jobs they apply for are given to women and minority applicants, some of whom are illegal aliens.

Labor Unions

Labor unions, which helped workers combat injustice in the sweatshop era, began to say who should work and who should not work.

In 1921 the unions succeeded in getting Congress to pass the deceptive Davis-Bacon Act. This act requires that government and federal-aided jobs pay the prevailing wages of the area in which the jobs are being done. In practice, it has encouraged some contractors to employ a few workers at high wages in order to raise the standard. This act adds some $15 to $20 billion a year to the taxpayers' bill.

Then another milestone was passed on June 28, 1938. The minimum wage law was passed. This wage, originally an entering wedge of 25 cents an hour, is now $3.35 an hour. Members of labor unions make much more than that. Yet, in every election campaign, labor unions demand a pledge from candidates that they will retain the minimum wage law if they want the votes of their members. Their purpose is monopoly. The high minimum wage prevents many would-be employers from training young men and women. This creates a shortage of skilled workers, allowing union labor to charge what it will. All of this adds greatly to inflation, welfare rolls, and high unemployment among young people seeking to enter the labor market.

Labor unions, with their contributions to candidates and their votes, have become a powerful factor in control of our government, and thus of American life. Immune from government interference, labor unions have engaged in strikes, with picketing, arson, vandalism, violence, and murder. Rising wages and their corollary, rising prices, have been forced higher and higher. A labor union chief, Raymond Donovan, was named Secretary of Labor in the Reagan Cabinet. In the 1984 Presidential election campaign, great labor unions endorsed Walter Mondale. Such endorsements carry many votes, and some $20 million in political contributions. Labor's purpose is to obligate their candidate to the unions, should he be elected. Special privileges for labor mean fewer jobs for non-union people and economic hardship for everyone.

In the struggle for government money and special privileges, other groups come in, such as the American Medical Association, feminist groups, the elderly, minorities, and many others.

When the apparent selection of the President shifted from the political boss system to the primary system (with its meaningless straw votes, its appeals to various factions), greater costs brought dependence upon the contributions of great financiers.

Fair Campaign Practice Act

Following the Watergate scandal, the people's demand for reform pushed Congress to pass the so-called "Fair Campaign Practice Act." It was signed into law October 15, 1974, and hailed as the most far-reaching reform in the nation's history. Our frontispiece of the signing shows President Ford surrounded by congressmen. The act was the answer to a politician's dream. It opened the floodgates of money to them.

The act provided:

1. For Presidential candidates the $1 check off from income taxes. This provides matching funds for eligible candidates' primaries, and some $20 million for the campaigns of each after nomination.

2. For Congressional candidates there is a great increase in the numbers of Political Action Committees, and their contributions.

Nowhere is there a selfless call for all factions to forego favored treatment and render all possible service for the good of the whole.

Present-Day Political Campaigns

The cost of campaigns for federal offices has become more and more expensive. Money is needed for organization of the campaign, for aides, stenographers, postage and telephone calls, travel, hotel bills, for newspapers, and television ads. The only people able and willing to contribute such large amounts of money are those who have a personal, financial interest in the candidates' future official actions.

Our Real Rulers

Through it all, almost unnoticed, the owners of the great banks and corporations have increased their control of our government and our nation, step by step. In their thirst for profit the demand is always for more, regardless of its effect upon this country and its people.

This book strips away the carefully woven veil behind which these financiers control and manipulate our government, and through this our nation and our lives. It reveals how, with precision planning, for profit, they throw us and our country into crisis after crisis. They have caused our terrible wars, the surrender of the Panama Canal, the Iranian hostage episode, the oil embargo, our great debts and high taxes, our recurring periods of inflation and depressions, our lengthening unemployment lines, and our growing welfare rolls. These things are not accidents or freaks of nature. All can be traced back to the financiers who put our public officials into office.

With money, not earned by service to the people, but created on computers through usurpation of the nation's monetary system, great financiers are in control. They have secured ownership of almost all productive property in the

United States, and hold bonds and legal claims for much of the rest.

Discharging their employees in America, they move their factories overseas and bring in their foreign-made goods, duty-free.

Our officials sell the nation's great natural resources to these power brokers: oil, gas, coal, timber, shale, and minerals, at an ultimate cost of nothing. (The small price originally paid is recovered in the final high pricing of the product. Consumers must pay all the traffic will bear for our natural resources, once they appear in manufactured form.)

Some early kings did try to preserve their nations. However, our present masters are citizens of the world who "think globally." They employ foreign-born agents to help them devise ways to internationalize the United States.

There is a way out of this dreadful morass of strain, subjugation, and fear.

There is a way to reclaim our government.

There is a way to reduce taxes to a small fraction of what they are today.

There is a way to start idle machines in our factories.

There is wealth enough in this nation for an adequate life for everyone.

My earlier book, *Honest Money*, tells how to reclaim our monetary system. This book tells how to reclaim our government and purify it.

With earnest effort, we, the people, can return to the *Constitution*, correct defects in our electoral system, and set our nation on the course envisioned by those who signed the *Declaration of Independence*, and those who gave their lives that this nation might live.

We will now leave generalities and see just who selects our President, and then turn to the election of our congressmen. We will see that the criterion of our federal officials, in every important act, is not what is right or wrong, nor what in the long run is best for the nation. It is, first of all, that which will please those who paid their election expenses and who might be giving them money or favors from time to time. Secondly, elected officials back programs that will bring them the most votes.

"And you shall not take a bribe, for a bribe blinds the clear-sighted and subverts the cause of the just"
(Exodus 23:8, *New American Standard Bible*).

CHAPTER 2

Presidential Elections

In recent Presidential campaigns, the taxpayers have provided matching funds to qualified candidates for primaries, and some $29.4 million for each nominee. It is probable that these contributions from nameless millions never receive a single thought of gratitude or commitment.

Some of the money to elect the President is made up of $1,000-a-plate dinners, and the like. These are not social affairs. The promoters are looking for tax breaks or some other favors. Ambassadorships and other appointments are commonly awarded to those who have raised or given money to successful candidates. Labor unions and other organizations bring in their contributions and pledge support, all for some special privileges.

Such isolated cases have been going on since men learned that they could safely bribe public officials. All of these are, however, small things. We are here concerned with actions far more dangerous.

Presidential candidates who have any hope of success are selected and nurtured by great financiers. As long as these contributors do not "communicate" with the candidate they can spend, in his behalf, as much as they choose. The 1980 Presidential election is estimated to have cost about $500 million (*The Christian Science Monitor,* 10/9/80).

The usual power broker employs lobbyists to persuade or bribe government officials. The great financiers, the internationalists, elect their own officials. They pay to put into office, or to keep in office, men who serve them by passing every law they request.

The Internationalists: Changing the Face of the United States

Though the United States of America is still revered in our national anthem as the land of the free, there has been a steady drift from a republic toward a welfare statist democracy, in which an increasingly greater number of citizens, once masters of their government, are now its dependents. Is this by chance or is it by design? And, if the latter, what is planned for the end?

Council on Foreign Relations (CFR)

After Senate rejection of the League of Nations, Colonel Edward House, its chief architect, assembled other one-world government fanatics, and, in 1921, incorporated the tax-free Council on Foreign Relations. The Rockefellers gave the building to house it. The Council was taken over by men of great wealth.

Membership in the Council is by invitation. Secrecy concerning all proceedings and discussion is a condition of membership.

The purpose of the Council on Foreign Relations has not been to hold meetings and give helpful advice. Its purpose, as shown by its actions, has been to gain control of the government and direct its course — for private profit and personal power.

David Rockefeller, retired chairman and chief executive of the Chase-Manhattan Bank, is chairman of the Council on Foreign Relations (CFR). Dan Smoot called this group "the invisible government" in his book by that title.

Government infiltration by the CFR has been effected through carefully selected, ambitious men — those who could be used. Elections of some are secured, financed by concerned members with mostly tax-free money. These officials appoint others. All, virtual agents of the Council's leaders, are placed in public office to further their goals. They hold the top decision-making jobs.

The United States Presidency and Vice Presidency have been handed from one CFR member to another as if these offices were personal chattel. For some forty years almost every President, Vice President, and the Secretaries of State, Defense, and Treasury were members of the CFR and allied groups controlled by the same financiers. It is likely that every important governmental policy is dictated by leaders of these groups.

President Nixon, selected, groomed, and largely financed by a member of the CFR (Nelson Rockefeller), appointed some 110 of the Council's members to government office.

The loyalty of many of these was, first and foremost, to serve the interests of those financiers who put them into office, and to whose employ they would return when their term of office was over.

It seems that nothing escapes the sharp eyes of men employed by the great financiers to attend to such things for them.

The following is just one example: In 1973 there came orders from the White House to sell much of the nation's stockpile of rare strategic metals — chromium, cobalt, titanium and the like. Sales of some $3 billion were made at bargain prices. Jack Anderson (4/15/76) completed the story. He stated that the White House saw to it that most sales were made to great corporations that had made contributions to Richard Nixon.

These metals, essential to the safety of our nation, must now be replaced by purchases from foreign cartels — at today's exorbitant prices. Most came from Africa where Russia is gaining control.

Many articles have dealt with our shortage of necessary minerals. In 1979 Congressman Jim Santini (D-NV) listed facts showing that our economy would come to a halt if the South African minerals were denied. He said, "I believe we are inviting possible calamity."

An informative article, "Strategic Minerals: The Invisible War," by Fred Warshopsky in *Reader's Digest* (February, 1981) repeats this dire warning.

The cost of a gyro housing for the F.B. III bomber has increased 14 times in ten years. This increase is mainly due to a rise in the price of beryllium.

The Bilderbergers
A Visitor From Abroad

Prince Bernhard, of the Netherlands, once a leader of the Bilderbergers, a worldwide group of financiers, came for a secret meeting at Lawrence Rockefeller's Woodstock Inn in Vermont, April 23, 24 and 25, 1971. The subject of the conference, Prince Bernhard said on arrival, would be the "Change in World Role of the United States." Henry Kissinger, member of the Council on Foreign Relations, and former secretary to Nelson Rockefeller, was at the meeting.

Bilderberger meetings are always secret. Reporters are

turned away with sub-machine guns.

In the wake of the Lockheed scandal and the charge that Prince Bernhard had accepted a million-dollar bribe, the Bilderbergers became quieter. Now they are becoming active again.

However such societies and associations may differ, they have one thing in common: they deal with the destiny of this nation in meetings from which almost all of our citizens and the press are excluded.

On August 15th President Nixon halted conversion of foreign-held United States dollars into gold. On December 18th the President announced an 8.57-percent devaluation of the dollar.

It has been charged that the advance notice of these acts and of other economic changes allowed members of the Bilderbergers to pocket as much as $20 million.

The Administration's stand against communism underwent an abrupt change. The President, who had lambasted communism and had continued the Vietnam War to contain it, now embraced its leaders.

President Nixon's detente, first with China and then with Russia, were then hailed as great examples of statesmanship. But were they? The American people are much worse off. In speaking of this on NBC April 4, 1974, the late Senator Henry Jackson (D-WA) said the cost to the American taxpayer of foreign aid to Russia was $8 billion, for which, he said, "We have received nothing."

The Trilateral Commission (TC)

Now we have the Trilateral Commission that, at present, supplies personnel for the executive branch of our central government.

This Commission is the brain child of David Rockefeller. It was organized and established in 1973 by Mr. Rockefeller's chief aide, Zbigniew Brzezinski. Its members were drawn from among the wealthiest and most powerful men in Western Europe, Japan and the United States and those they could use. The American Branch has 76 members. The Commission is financed by grants from great foundations and great corporations, profits from its own investments, and gifts from concerned individuals, all or nearly all tax-free. The Rockefeller Foundation and the Rockefeller Brothers Fund furnish $230,000, and David Rockefeller gives $150,000 a year.

Dean Rusk was close to the Rockefellers. He was director of the Rockefeller Foundation until he became Secretary of State. Later, as a professor in Georgia, he had ample time to observe Jimmy Carter. Jimmy Carter was a master politician. Advertising himself as a "born-again Christian," he capitalized on an image of truthfulness, frequently saying, "I will never lie to you."

George Franklin, coordinator of the Trilaterals, went down to interview Jimmy Carter. Mr. Carter was taken in as a founding member. He met David Rockefeller.

Jimmy Carter learned fast. Next we find him delivering his "World Order" speech before the Council on Foreign Relations. Such a man could be useful to the leaders of the Trilateral. They selected him for the Presidency.

Mr. Rockefeller sent his aide, Zbigniew Brzezinski, to stand by Mr. Carter's side and travel with him during the campaign.

The Trilateral Presidency: "Jimmy" Carter

Resigning from official membership in the Trilateral Commission upon taking office were President "Jimmy"

Carter, Vice President "Fritz" Mondale, Secretary of State Cyrus Vance, Secretary of Defense Harold Brown, and Head of National Security Zbigniew Brzezinski — the entire foreign policy and national defense team. *U.S. News & World Report* (5/22/78) listed 18 Trilaterals in top positions of the federal government. Roughly another hundred were appointed from David Rockefeller's other, older, elitist Council on Foreign Relations (CFR) or similar mushrooming groups, such as the Aspen Institute for Humanistic Studies.

It seems that every President must have a slogan. Mr. Carter chose "Human Rights." By this he meant that pro-Western governments which violated human rights would be punished, while the same or worse oppression in communist countries would be blandly tolerated.

Those who believe he betrayed the constituency that elected him are naive. The night he accepted the Democratic nomination for President at the party convention in 1976, he said the following:

> ". . . This calls for nothing less than a sustained architectural effort to shape an *international framework of peace* within which our own ideals gradually can become a *global* reality. . . . To those *nation-states* that wish to compete with us, I say that we neither fear competition nor see it as an obstacle to wider cooperation . . ." (italics added to identify TC-CFR catchwords — Ed.).

It is seldom that the true philosophy and aims of a politician are laid bare so early in a campaign. Yet a year later President Carter was still anxious to bow to the idol-dream of the internationalists who had put him in office. The message he wrote and placed in a spacecraft then was not for earthlings, but for the inhabitants of a planet of some distant star. The message follows:

"The White House, June 16, 1977.

"This Voyager spacecraft was constructed by the United States of America. We are a community of 240 million human beings among the more than 4 billion who inhabit the planet Earth. We human beings are still divided into nation-states, but these states are rapidly becoming a single global civilization."

Dr. Anthony C. Sutton, author of *Trilaterals Over Washington,* called the TC placement of Jimmy Carter in the White House "the ultimate *coup de grace* in history . . . the total domination of the Executive Branch of the U.S. Government." Sutton also said, "It is socialist revolution by stealth, rather than by blood in the streets, but revolution just the same. Trilateralism is the current operational vehicle for a corporate socialist takeover."

President Carter, selected and influenced by the Trilateral bankers who were financing the USSR, gave the Soviets some all-important oil drills, the giant magnet of atomic research which had taken years to design and build, and our minute ball bearings (vital to their rocket guidance system). Worst of all, he decimated our military superiority already severely weakened by earlier CFR members, Robert Strange McNamara and Henry Kissinger, in their successive roles as Secretary of Defense under the Democrats and Secretary of State under Republican administrations, respectively.

Carter also vetoed the B-1 bomber, and delayed the cruise missile, neutron bomb, and new ships for the Navy. In pursuit of the "Better Red Than Dead" MAD doctrine ("Mutual Assured Destruction"), he fostered the SALT II Treaty — the last scrap of paper the USSR would ever need. Although he was unable to get the Senate to ratify it, he abode by its provisions as long as he was in office. NPL, the publisher of this book, received numerous testimonies of eye-witness observers to concrete being poured into the ballistic-missile tubes of nuclear submarines at Norfolk, Virginia. When these observers asked why such an incredible dismantling of our SSBN's had been ordered, they were told that Carter was complying with the non-ratified SALT II Treaty!

However, history will probably show that Carter's most weakening, dangerous deed was the surrender of our canal in Panama — with treaties that were never agreed to by Panama in the same final form as ratified by the U.S. Senate. It is one of those cases where truth is far stranger than fiction.

The Panama Canal

Have you wondered why Jimmy Carter, a peanut dealer and once the Governor of Georgia, in the first days of his Presidency, would select as his prime objective the surrender of the Panama Canal? Anyone who will study the Canal's history will find that the Canal belonged to the United States. It was bought and paid for with American treasure and blood. There was no moral or human rights question there.

Panama, Colombia, Equador, and Venezuela were Spanish colonies. They joined forces in a successful rebellion. The four then entered a confederacy. Equador and Venezuela withdrew in 1829 and 1830. Mistreated, Panama tried to withdraw. Colombia, sixteen times greater in size, would not permit this. Panama was kept in subjugation for nearly 80 years. Several times she revolted and tried to secede. Near the end of the last time — the War of a Thousand Days — she appealed to the United States for help.

The French began work on the Canal in 1880, and gave

up 19 years later. The United States gave the French $40 million dollars for their franchise. Although we offered to pay Colombia, she would not accept the transfer. Responding to Panama's request for aid, we paid the Panamanian government $10 million, and separately paid every Panama landowner who held property in the Canal Zone. We guaranteed Panama's independence and agreed to pay her $250,000 a year, a large sum in those days. Our Navy stopped Colombia from invading Panama. This Treaty with Panama was signed February 26, 1904. The Canal was opened August 15, 1914. Colombia held a grudge. This was settled in 1922. We paid Colombia $25 million dollars, and gave her certain land transportation concessions. Colombia acknowledged that she was satisfied and recognized Panama.

Thus we paid the French, Panama and its citizens, and Colombia, and dug the canal. It was ours. Through the years we raised the payment to Panama to $2.5 million annually. Since the Canal treaties we now have to pay $75 million a year in tolls and rentals.

During the Carter campaign we read many newspapers, news periodicals and viewed the newscasts. Not once did we see a word or hint that Mr. Carter planned to give the Canal away. Yet, immediately after the election he brought forth a mature, forceful plan to do just that.

Striking at once, before the Presidential honeymoon had time to cool, President Carter appointed Sol Linowitz, a member of the Trilaterals, as chief negotiator, and brought up the Canal Treaty — without "the advice and consent of the Senate" (as provided in the *Constitution).* The President signed the Treaty in a spectacular ceremony attended by the heads of many other countries. This was calculated to force, and did force, the Senate to fall in line and surrender this vital link in our national defense. Just why would President

Carter do this? Consider the following:

George Franklin, coordinator of the Trilateral Commission *(U.S. News & World Report,* May 22, 1979), put it this way: "It is clear that President Carter received a very considerable foreign policy education from the Commission. Carter acknowledges that Brzezinski in his capacity as director of the Trilateral Commission was his top mentor in foreign affairs."

And then the following quoted from David Rockefeller, in *The Miami Herald,* April 20, 1980:

> "Coming from Georgia . . . Carter had very little international exposure or even national exposure. Carter found in Trilateral a lot of very able people representing different views that he needed in government."

It was not just President Carter then that gave the Canal away. Behind the surrender was the mind and hand of the Trilateralists.

Those Trilateralists who counseled President Carter to give the Canal away should have known that Panama may go communistic, and that Russia will fight to preserve and control all little communistic countries, and that in this case she may control the Canal.

The terms laid down in the treaty seem terms dictated to a nation defeated in war.

Perhaps the most humiliating of these terms is the provision that the United States, a great sovereign nation, is forbidden to build another canal without the permission of Panama.

But why the Canal?

Panama shipping and banking laws are very lax. United States capitalists, to take advantage of this, have registered many of their ships there. They also have great oil refineries, great banks and other investments there. At the time of the treaty, newspapers told of the Chase-Manhattan Bank and other great New York banks' huge loans to Panama — how the money we paid to Panama went straight to these great banks in payment of interest on those loans. They also reported that Panama could not pay the principal. Now, after the Treaty, we will pay Panama between $45 and $70 million a year. With these payments Panama can keep the loans from default.

Some thirty-one Trilateralists sit on boards of banks in Panama.

The Embassy Hostages in Iran

Like Panama, Iran is another area where the international bankers have made huge investments.

Iran suffered terribly under the Shah's rule. "The jails were filled with thousands of political prisoners, and SAVAK was universally reviled for its tactics of terror and torture." "No country in the world," concluded Amnesty International in 1975, "has a worse record in human rights than Iran."

The Iranian people blamed the United States for forcing the Shah upon them. Early in 1979 they stormed the American Embassy — and were repulsed.

Our former Ambassador to Iran, William Sullivan, has said that our State Department was repeatedly warned that if the Shah was admitted to the United States, the Iranians would take the Embassy personnel hostage.

David Rockefeller and Henry Kissinger pressured President Carter to admit the Shah.

Finally, ignoring the rights of this nation to a friendly relationship with Iran, our need for oil, the freedom and perhaps the lives of the people in the Embassy, as well as the possibility of armed conflict, President Carter admitted the Shah. The Embassy was stormed and its personnel taken hostage.

The President then froze some $11 billion of Iranian assets.

The President immediately brought the hostage question into politics for his own advantage. Month after month he harped on this string. He allowed the hostage issue to subordinate everything else. Columnist David Broder quoted a letter from abroad: "You have no idea — how unsettled the whole world finds the spectacle of the American President on whose judgment we all rely, allowing his schedule, his activities, his policies and his dealings with his Allies to be dictated by the gang of hoodlums holding your people in Tehran."

The year 1980 may well go down in history as the "Year of the Hostages." Every newscast, every newspaper, every day seemed devoted to the hostages and the obtaining of their release. There was far more concern for the Embassy personnel held hostage by Leftists than for all our soldiers in all our wars.

News today is flashed around the world. Do those in other countries who see and read it know of the stranglehold financiers have on our government? Do they realize the American taxpayer works over five months to pay his taxes? (Serfs in the Middle Ages worked only three months of the year for their masters' portion!) Do nationals of other countries have reservations about our brand of capitalism?

It is hard for the average television-watcher, at home or abroad, to realize the extent of collusion between Big Banking, Big Business, Big Government, and Big Media. American visitors to Iran during the hostage crisis told the incredible facts of the daily "media events." Throngs of apparently bored Iranians would gather in front of the American Embassy where the hostages were being held, chatting together until the American news teams with their television cameras showed up. Then, suddenly, a few agitators would whip the crowd into a frenzy while the cameras churned away!

Later, newscasts featured great throngs of people rushing about in the streets, carrying banners, waving their clenched fists, damning America, burning our flag. Doubtless they are as frustrated as we are at banker-support for corrupt and despotic rulers who kickback their natural resources to those same bankers — the price demanded to keep such puppets in power.

That was what Rep. George Hansen (R-ID) discovered when he went to Iran. He took time to talk to the people outside the Embassy and tell them how little the American people agree with policies forged on Wall Street.

Congressman Hansen's investigation disclosed the fact that before the Shah was brought into the United States, State Department officials became involved in the process of determining the feasibility of freezing Iran's assets. He also discovered that the State Department had been warned that the Embassy personnel would be in danger if the Shah were allowed to enter America.

Since Iran retained its sovereign national immunity against private lawsuits, no grounds existed for such a freeze until the contrived crisis came about!

Several times, success in negotiations for the hostages' release seemed promising; yet always some difficulty arose. The Shah's last day in Panama, which took him after political pressure forced him from the U.S., was no exception. Authorities in Iran asked for a few hours' extension of time to get the hostages under army protection: a condition for the Shah's arrest. Release of the hostages seemed imminent. Suddenly a large jet plane whisked the ailing Shah to Egypt, where he later died — but not before he spoke of massive betrayal by the international bankers who had put him in power and kept him there until he outlived his usefulness to them.

Once the Shah was in Egypt, money was mentioned. Apparently President Carter had to have the bankers' permission before making a successful monetary offer for the release of the hostages. The offer was to return a part of Iran's money, not all.

When Iran's assets in big multinational banks were frozen because of the orchestrated hostage crisis, they were worth some $11 billion. In the settlement for the release of the hostages, Iran received $2.8 billion; the bankers still held $7.977 billion of the Shah's wealth.

At later trials in the United States and Europe, there were various settlements. On August 22, 1981, it was announced that more money had been released to Iran — after enough had been retained to satisfy all creditors.

Several lessons can be learned from Carter's Trilateral Presidency and the Shah's puppet regime for Wall Street banking and oil interests. Both men became expendable once they had "delivered" for their secret masters.

President Carter used every means at his disposal to remain in office. After endorsements and before primaries he handed out billions of dollars of taxpayer money.

But President Carter had played his part. His indifference to American interests had offended every patriotic citizen. Those who put him in office knew he could no longer fool the people, so they looked elsewhere. The hostages returned to America during the very hour that Ronald Reagan was being inaugurated as America's 40th President!

Are we to believe that "luck" always favors bankers, or are we to believe the following?

"In politics nothing happens by accident. If it happens at all, you can bet it was planned that way."
— *Franklin D. Roosevelt*

Ronald Reagan: A Republican
"A Change Might Help"

The Trilateral Commission "makes no bones about it," said TC Coordinator to *U.S. News & World Report* (5/22/79). It recruits only people interested in promoting "closer international cooperation." In other words, it does not accept as members men who believe in a sovereign, unified, independent United States of America. It makes every effort to exclude such men from government.

It was evident early in the 1980 Presidential campaign that CFR-TC member George Bush was the preferred candidate of the elitists. However, the people wanted Ronald Reagan, who had vast conservative and populist support. Therefore, "when you can't lick 'em, join 'em!"

Right after the New Hampshire primary, Reagan fired his campaign manager, John Sears, and said he had money only for one or two more state primaries. Then he hired CFR member William Casey to take Sears' place, and put him in charge of the C.I.A. after he was elected.

Almost at once he had plenty of money. He also had, at his disposal, a large jet airplane and crew of assistants. Aboard as chief advisor was CFR-TC member Casper Weinberger, a long-time aide, but also a close associate of David Rockefeller.

Soon Ronald Reagan sounded the note of the internationalist. He said that if elected President, he would open the boundaries between the United States, Mexico, and Canada. As soon as he was nominated, he named George Bush, his chief rival for the nomination, as his running mate. Along with Bush, he must have been required to take James Baker as the most powerful of the "big three" of his White House staff. Baker was not only Bush's campaign manager; he had also worked against Reagan at the Republican convention four years before, making deals with Reagan delegates to get them to switch to Ford.

Reagan's own basic, conservative-populist support became disillusioned and bewildered as Baker-Rockefeller policies prevailed at the White House. *Conservative Digest* devoted its entire July 1982 issue to the subject, "Has Reagan Deserted the Conservatives?"

After Mr. Reagan was elected President, he appointed 73 CFR or TC members. Many top aides were, and are, very close to the Rockefellers, as well as Nixon, Ford and Kissinger. His Cabinet is chiefly composed of great industrialists. Several are very wealthy. Almost at once we learn that David Rockefeller is speaking for the new President in Argentina. And we find Henry Kissinger speaking for him in the Middle East. Later Kissinger was appointed to head a Commission on Central America, where the Rockefellers have many chestnuts in the fire.

Our government, and therefore the nation, is still controlled by the same men.

President Reagan had promised a tax cut, which he said would lessen the people's burden; yet his first meaningful act was to begin to favor those who had put him in office. He deregulated the price of the rest of the oil. This results in an increase of $20 billion a year in windfall profit taxes, which, together with the oil companies' great profits, are taken from the people. The tax cut that followed, for most people, did not nearly offset this added burden.

In one of his State of the Union speeches to Congress, President Reagan stated: "Our own economic well-being is inextricably linked to the world economy, and we will continue to work closely with the industrialized democracies of Europe and Japan with the International Monetary Fund — to ensure it has adequate resources to help bring the world economy back to strong, non-inflationary growth.''

The money is to come from our middle class taxpayer, either in cash or to be added to his debt.

In the spring of 1983 our national monetary system and our economy were in sad array. One might think that our elected officials would meet in our capital to decide our course — but no. Our government officials, placed into their positions by great international financiers, left these important decisions to such bankers.

On April 17, 1983, the Trilateral Commission met, not in this country, but in Rome.

On April 29, 1983, an allied group, the Club of Rome, met in Geneva. Since no earlier mention of this organization has been made, a brief description is in order. It was founded in 1965 by Aurelio Peccei of Italy's Fiat Motor Company. Peccei was indoctrinated at the Tavistock Institute in England, "the mother of all think tanks," according to *World Economic Review* (January 1984). This periodical also says that after Peccei's Tavistock training, "he recruited all of the top members of NATO into the new controlling body, the top conspiratorial oversight body in the world."

The Club of Rome has published its goals in a book available in many public libraries: *Limits to Growth,* by Donzella Meadows et al. It favors programs that would drastically reduce earth's population and deindustrialize the Western nations, especially the U.S. This strange "Club" authorized the study which produced the "Global 2,000 Report," a program for genocide.

On May 13, 1983, the Bildebergers, closely associated

with the other elite groups and having interlocking members, met at Montebello, Quebec.

The discussions of these three conferences were, as usual, barred from press coverage. However, since the government leaders of seven leading industrial nations met soon afterward, it is fairly safe to assume that they were there to implement decisions already made by the financiers in the other three conferences.

On May 28, 1983, President Reagan and other heads of state from Western nations met in Williamsburg, Virginia. Their stated purpose was to implement the World Bank in its "aid to undeveloped countries." This is done by forcing taxpayers of the United States and elsewhere to furnish money to Lesser Developed Countries (LDC's) so that they can pay their loans, plus interest, to the banks. The LDC's also need money to pay for the financiers' manufactured goods, made in the U.S. and in other countries.

President Reagan promised $50 billion from the U.S. to the IMF, according to *Spotlight* (6/13/83). Before 1983 was over, $8.4 billion had been appropriated by Congress for the IMF; $15 billion for the Export-Import Bank; $7 billion to the multilateral development bank. Thus, an unbelievable $30 billion was extorted from the American people, whose flood of mail and phone calls of protest to Congress met with deaf ears. Why this should be so will be much more clear to the reader who studies the four-page chart at the end of this chapter. A patriot in Texas has compiled this research identifying CFR-TC members in government, industry, the media and organized labor. The name and address of his organization, and how to get more data, are included at the end of the report. Since the material is deliberately not copyrighted, the reader is free to photocopy anything from those four pages in any quantity.

The New York Times (5/1/83) stated *before* Williamsburg that President Reagan would "ask Congress to consolidate import-export operations in a new Department — that of International Trade, which would take over functions now performed at Commerce."

Step by step, there is always pressure to increase the size of the bureaucracy and overshadow our national institutions with One-World ones.

The 1984 Presidential Election

As this book goes to press, we look forward to the 1984 Presidential election.

We have seen President Reagan's program. Is there, in the coming election, a chance for change — for improvement — for electing a President who will care for the country as a whole, and not be interested in advancing any particular faction of it?

Walter Mondale, one apparent alternative, was former President Jimmy Carter's Vice President. The great international financiers put Mr. Carter into office, and he chose Mr. Mondale. Johnny Stewart of F.R.E.E. (source of the chart at the end of this chapter) says he was both a CFR & TC member.

Walter Mondale was a major speaker at the fifth Congress of the International Humanist and Ethical Union in August of 1970. At that time he said, "Although I have never formally joined a humanist society, I think I am a member by inheritance. My preacher father was a humanist ... and I grew up on a very rich diet of humanism from him."

Mr. Mondale has said nothing about controlling great corporations in their monopoly over the necessities of life; there is not a word about control of international financiers' manipulations of the nation's money and economy for private profit; there is nothing said about the carrying of American factories to foreign lands and the resulting long lines of the unemployed.

Instead, Mr. Mondale has played upon the needs of the victims of these injustices. In his desire for office, his thirst for power, and wealth, he has, like Mr. Carter before him, become all things to all people.

Mr. Mondale has made promises of special privileges to labor unions, to teachers, to the elderly, to blacks, and to homosexuals.

In Puerto Rico, where half of the people are on our taxpayers' food stamps, Mr. Mondale stated that if elected he will abide by their wishes — statehood, if they desire it.

The choice of candidates in the 1984 Presidential election shows the necessity of a return to the *Constitution*, as outlined in this book. The *Constitution* may be read in Appendix C.

We know little of Gary Hart. The night of the New Hampshire primary a commentator said Hart had little money. Mr. Hart spoke of: "I have it now." He speaks of world cooperation, and says he is against tariffs.

A Return to the *Constitution*

The incidences related in this chapter would not have occurred if we had followed the Constitutional method of choosing our President. This growing danger can be stopped by an order of the Supreme Court, or by a simple act of Congress. This is made clear in "The Solution."

The CFR-TC four-page chart now follows. It should convince even the most skeptical of how tight the interlocking control of the power brokers is. Millions of these charts have already been distributed. Many other books and periodicals document the existence of this "invisible government."

The rest of *Honest Government* will document many specific instances where multinational banks and corporations have robbed the hardworking middle class to line their own coffers and strengthen their iron grip on the whole world.

THE TRILATERAL CONNECTION

DAVID ROCKEFELLER
CHAIRMAN OF THE
COUNCIL ON FOREIGN RELATIONS
58 E. 68th St., New York, NY 10021
Phone (212) 734-0400

NORTH AMERICAN CHAIRMAN OF
The TRILATERAL COMMISSION
345 E. 46th St., New York, NY 10017
Phone (212) 661-1180

★ **CFR:** Indicates past or present membership in the Council on Foreign Relations

★ **TC:** Indicates past or present membership in the Trilateral Commission

★ "The Council on Foreign Relations is the American Branch of a society which originated in England...(and)...believes national boundaries should be obliterated and one-world rule established...

"The Trilateral Commission is international...(and)...is intended to be the vehicle for multinational consolidation of the commercial and banking interests by seizing control of the political government of the United States." **WITH NO APOLOGIES,** Senator Barry Goldwater.

RONALD REAGAN
(non member)

NATIONAL SECURITY COUNCIL

GEORGE BUSH — CFR TC
VICE PRESIDENT

ALEXANDER HAIG — CFR
GEORGE P. SCHULTZ — CFR
SECRETARY OF STATE

C. WEINBERGER — CFR TC
SECRETARY OF DEFENSE

GEN. DAVID JONES — CFR
CHAIRMAN, JOINT CHIEFS OF STAFF

WILLIAM CASEY — CFR
CENTRAL INTELLIGENCE AGENCY

ROBERT McNAMARA — CFR
INTERNATIONAL BANK FOR RECONSTRUCTION & DEVELOPMENT

W.B. DALE — CFR
INTERNATIONAL MONETARY FUND

H.B. CHENERY — CFR
WORLD BANK

FEDERAL RESERVE SYSTEM
(Past & Present — Partial Listing)

Paul Volcker	CFR TC
Anthony M. Solomon	CFR TC
Emmett J. Rice	CFR
Henry Wallich	CFR
Donald C. Platten	CFR
Robert H. Knight, Esq.	CFR
Steven Muller	CFR
Gerald D. Hines	CFR
John V. James	CFR
Andrew R. Brimmer	CFR TC
George Weyerhaeuser	CFR TC
Henry Woodbridge, Jr.	CFR TC

SPECIAL ADVISERS TO NATO SECURITY COUNCIL

DAVID ROCKEFELLER — CFR TC

HENRY KISSINGER — CFR TC

TREASURY
(Past & Present — Partial Listing)

Donald Regan	CFR
John Heimann	CFR
C.D. Lord	CFR
William Simon	CFR
Michael Blumenthal	CFR TC
C. Fred Bergsten	CFR
Anthony M. Solomon	CFR TC
Arnold Nachmanoff	CFR
Helen B. Junz	CFR
Richard Fisher	CFR
Roger Altman	CFR
George Pratt Schultz	CFR

DEPARTMENT OF STATE

Alexander Haig, Sec. of State CFR	Raymond Platig, CFR	Richard Blomfield (Portugal) CFR
George Shultz (replaced Haig) CFR	(Intelligence, Research)	Charles Bray, III (Senegal) CFR
(Shultz is a director of the CFR)	Myer Rashish, CFR	Arthur Burns (W. Germany) CFR
Walter Stoessel, Jr. CFR	(Economic Affairs)	Horace Dawson (Botswana) CFR
(Under Sec.)	Paul Wolfowitz, CFR	Angier Duke (Morocco) CFR
Carol Baumann, (Research) CFR	(Policy Planning)	James E. Goodby (Finland) CFR
Richard Burt, CFR	James Spain CFR	Arthur Hartman (U.S.S.R.) CFR
(Politico Military affairs)		Deane Hinton (El Salvador) CFR
Mark Feldman, (Legal) CFR		Samuel Lewis (Israel) CFR
Ann Hollick CFR	**AMBASSADORS**	James Lowenstein (Luxmbg.) CFR
(Policy Assessment)	Jeane Kirkpatrick (U.N.) CFR	William Luers (Venezuela) CFR
Robert Hormats CFR	Richard Petree (U.N.) CFR	Ronald Palmer (Malaysia) CFR
(Economics, Business)	Morton Abramowitz (Thailand) CFR	Thomas Pickering (Nigeria) CFR
Edward Morse CFR	Michael Armacost (Phillipines) CFR	Maxwell Rabb (Italy) CFR
(Internal Energy Policy)	Alfred Atherton (Egypt) CFR	Ronald Spiers (Pakistan) CFR
Michael Peay CFR	Harry Barnes, Jr. (India) CFR	R. Strausz-Hupe (Turkey) CFR
(Legal, Law Enforcement)	Harry Bergold, Jr. (Hungary) CFR	Terence Todman (Spain) CFR

BUREAU OF INTER AMERICAN AFFAIRS
(Cuba, Nicaragua, Panama, ElSalvador)
* Luigi Einaudi, Director, Policy Planning CFR

BUREAU OF AFRICAN AFFAIRS
(Rhodesia, Angola, South Africa)
* Chester Crocker, Assistant Secretary CFR

BUREAU OF EAST ASIAN & PACIFIC AFFAIRS
(Vietnam, Laos, Cambodia, Thailand, Korea, Taiwan)
* Michael Armacost, Dep. Asst. Secretary CFR
* Frederick Brown, Director CFR
* John Negroponte, Dept. Asst. Secretary CFR

BUREAU OF EUROPEAN AFFAIRS
Lawrence Eagleburger, Asst. Secretary CFR
Sandra Vogelgesang, Policy Planning CFR

BUREAU OF INTERNATIONAL ORGANIZATION AFFAIRS
Elliott Abrams, Asst. Secretary CFR

*PLEASE NOTE: These CFR/TC members head State Department bureaus where dramatic shifts in American foreign policy appear to work against allies of the United States and in favor of revolutionary forces.

STATE GOVERNORS
(INCLUDING FORMER GOVERNORS)

Reuben Askew	Gov. of FL.	CFR
Bruce Babbitt	Gov. of AZ.	CFR TC
George Busbee	Gov. of GA.	TC
James Earl Carter	Gov. of GA.	TC
Daniel J. Evans	Gov. of WA.	TC
Robert Graham	Gov. of FL.	CFR
John D. Rockefeller IV	Gov. of W.A.	CFR TC
William W. Scranton	Gov. of PA.	CFR TC
James C. Thompson, Jr.	Gov. of IL.	CFR

T. TANNENWALD, Jr. **CFR** U.S. TAX COURT	JAMES DUFFY **CFR** POSTAL RATE COMM.	ABBOTT WASHBURN **CFR** FEDERAL COMMUNICATIONS COMMISSION	GEORGE DALLEY **CFR** CIVIL AERONAUTICS BOARD

To Whom Do Americans Owe Allegiance?

U.S. MILITARY
Past & Present CFR/TC Members (partial listing)

ALLIED SUPREME COMMANDERS	
49-52 Eisenhower	CFR
52-53 Ridgeway	CFR
53-56 Gruenther	CFR
56-63 Norstad	CFR
63-69 Lemnitzer	CFR
69-74 Goodpaster	CFR
74-79 Haig	CFR
80-	

SECRETARIES OF DEFENSE	
57-59 McElroy	CFR
59-61 Gates	CFR
61-68 McNamara	CFR
69-73 Laird	CFR
73 Richardson	CFR TC
75-77 Rumsfeld	CFR
77- Brown	CFR TC
80- Weinberger	CFR TC

DEP. SEC. OF DEFENSE	
Frank Carlucci	CFR

UNDER SEC. OF DEFENSE	
Fred Ikle	CFR
GEN. Stillwell (Ret.)	CFR

ASST. SEC. of DEFENSE	
Lawrence Korb	CFR

SUPERINTENDENTS U.S. MILITARY ACADEMY AT WEST POINT	
60-63 Westmoreland	CFR
63-66 Lampert	CFR
66-68 Bennett	CFR
70-74 Knowlton	CFR
74-77 Berry	CFR
77- Goodpaster	CFR

PRESIDENT, NATIONAL DEFENSE UNIVERSITY	
LG Robert Gard, Jr.	CFR

SECRETARY OF THE NAVY	
John Lehman, Jr.	CFR

CHIEF OF STAFF, USAF	
GEN Lou Allen, Jr.	CFR

JOINT STAFF	
VADM Thor Hanson	CFR
LG Paul Gorman	CFR

MILITARY FELLOWS	
Army MG T. Ayers	CFR
AF COL K. Baker	CFR
Army LG S. Berry	CFR
Army BG Z. Bradford	CFR
Navy CAP J. Dewenter	CFR
Army Col A. Dewey	CFR
Navy Capt H. Fiske	CFR
AF Col E. Foote	CFR
Army LG R. Gard	CFR
AF MG R. Ginsburgh	CFR
Army BG M. Green	CFR
AF COL R. Head	CFR
AF BG T. Julian	CFR
Navy CAPT H. Kerr	CFR
AF COL I. Klette	CFR
Navy CAPT R. Kurth	CFR
AF Lt. COL J. Levy	CFR
Army COL G. Loeffke	CFR
AF LG G. Loving	CFR
AF COL M. McPeak	CFR
Navy CAPT R. Miale	CFR
AF LG J. Pfautz	CFR
AF COL L. Pfeiffer	CFR
Navy CAPT S. Ring	CFR
AF COL M. Sanders	CFR
Army COL J. Sewall	CFR
Navy RADM C. Tesh	CFR
AF COL F. Thayer	CFR
Army MG J. Thompson	CFR
AF MG W. Usher	CFR
Army GEN S. Walker	CFR
Navy Rad.R. Welander	CFR
AF COL J. Wolcott	CFR
Navy CAPT Gentry	CFR
AF COL T. Eggers	CFR

ADDITIONAL MILITARY	
MG R.C. Bowman	CFR
BG F. Brown	CFR
LT COL W. Clark	CFR
CAPT Ralph Crosby	CFR
ADM Wm. Crowe	CFR
COL P. Dawkins	CFR
VADM Thor Hanson	CFR
COL W. Hauser	CFR
COL B. Hosmer	CFR
MAJ R. Kimmitt	CFR
CAPT F. Klotz	CFR
GEN W. Knowlton	CFR
VADM J. Lee	CFR
CAPT T.T. Lupfer	CFR
COL D. Mead	CFR
MG Jack Merritt	CFR
GEN E. Meyer	CFR
COL Wm. E. Odom	CFR
COL L. Olvey	CFR
COL Geo. K. Osborn	CFR
MG J. Pustay	CFR
CAPT P.A. Putignano	CFR
LG E.L. Rowny	CFR
CAPT Gary Sick	CFR
MG J. Siegle	CFR
MG De Witt Smith	CFR
BG Perry Smith	CFR
LTG Wm. Y. Smith	CFR
COL W. Taylor	CFR
MG J.N. Thompson	CFR
RADM C.A.H. Trost	CFR
ADM S. Turner	CFR
MG J. Welch	CFR
GEN J. Wickham	CFR

BANKRUPTING AMERICA!

CFR MEMBERSHIP BREAKDOWN
(1980-'81 Yearbook)

Government	260 (12%)
Business	650 (30%)
Lawyers	216 (10%)
Scholars & Educators	411 (19%)

303 (14%) are involved in non-profit foundations which fund America's enemies at home and abroad, yet appear to be immune from congressional investigation.

MALCOLM BALDRIGE
CFR
SEC. OF COMMERCE

PRESIDENTS COMMISSION ON EXECUTIVE EXCHANGE

David Rockefeller — CFR TC
Willard Butcher, Pres., CFR
(Chase Manhattan Bank)
Thornton Bradshaw, CFR
(Pres., Atlantic Richfield)
John McKinley, Pres., CFR
(Texaco Oil Co.)
Ruben Mettler, CFR
(Chairman, TRW)
John Whitehead, CFR
(Goldman, Sachs & Co.)
Marina v. N. Whitman, CFR TC
(General Motors Corp.)

CHRYSLER

Jerome Holland	CFR
Najeeb Halaby	CFR
Tom Killefer	CFR
J. R. Dilworth	CFR
Gabriel Hauge	CFR

GENERAL MOTORS

Reuben R. Jensen	CFR
Roger B. Smith	CFR
Marina N. Whitman	CFR TC

INTERNATIONAL

Andrew Brimmer	CFR TC
Brooks McCormick	CFR

FORD MOTOR CO.

Donald E. Petersen	CFR
Carter L. Burgess	CFR
Clifton Wharton, Jr.	CFR
Philip Caldwell	TC
Arjay Miller	TC

TEXAS INSTRUMENTS

Mark Shepherd, Jr.	CFR TC
J. Fred Bucy, Jr.	CFR

CITIBANK

Walter B. Wriston	CFR
G.A. Costanzo	CFR
Hans Angermueller	CFR
George J. Vojta	CFR
Lief H. Olsen	CFR
Thomas Theobald	CFR

Who Is Responsible For:
Recession — Depression

Influence or Control of Money, Mail, Media, Military, IRS/Tax Courts, Commerce, Energy, Unions, Domestic and Foreign Policy, etc. Provides an Apparent Opportunity for Massive Fraud, Robbery, and Control of the American People!

The U.S. government and private debt money system are *not* "out of control". They are scientifically controlled by the CFR/TC!

EXXON / STANDARD

Clifton Garvin, Jr.	CFR
Jack Bennett	CFR
W. Bromery	CFR
J.G. Clark	CFR
J.E. Dean	CFR
J.K. Jamieson	CFR
Franklin Long	CFR
George Piercy	CFR
Otto von Amerongen	TC
Stephen Stamas	CFR
J.A. Armstrong	CFR
George M. Keller	CFR
Carla Hills	TC
David Packard	TC
Charles M. Pigott	CFR
George Weyerhaeuser	TC

MOBIL

Rawleigh Warner, Jr.	CFR
William Tavoulareas	CFR
Lewis Branscomb	CFR
Howard L. Clark	CFR
Alan Greenspan	CFR
George McGhee	CFR
Lee L. Morgan	CFR TC
Herbert Schmertz	CFR
Eleanor B. Sheldon	CFR

ATLANTIC RICHFIELD

Robert O. Anderson	CFR
T.F. Bradshaw	CFR
Phillip M. Hawley	TC
Robert Ingersoll	CFR
John B.M. Place	CFR
Frank Stanton	CFR

TEXACO

Maurice F. Granville	CFR
John K. McKinley	CFR
Robert V. Roosa	CFR TC

GULF

James E. Lee	CFR

SHELL

John F. Bookout	CFR

OCCIDENTAL

A. Robert Abboud	CFR

GENERAL ELECTRIC

Reginald H. Jones	CFR
John F. Burlingame	TC

AT&T

Edward W. Carter	CFR
Jerome H. Holland	CFR
Juanita M. Kreps	CFR
Peter E. Haas	CFR
William A. Hewitt	CFR TC
Rawleigh Warner, Jr.	CFR

CATERPILLAR

L. L. Morgan	CFR
R. S. Ingersoll	CFR TC

JOHN DEERE

William A. Hewitt	CFR TC

CHASE MANHATTAN CORP.

David Rockefeller	CFR TC
Willard C. Butcher	CFR
William S. Ogden	CFR
Robert R. Douglass	CFR
John C. Haley	CFR
Charles F. Barber	CFR
J. R. Dilworth	CFR
Richard M. Furlaud	CFR
Theodore Hesburgh	CFR
Ralph Lazarus	CFR
Edmund T. Pratt, Jr.	CFR
S. Bruce Smart, Jr.	CFR
Wm. T. Coleman, Jr.	CFR TC
James L. Ferguson	CFR
Alexander Haig, Jr.	CFR
John D. Macomber	CFR
Leo Martinuzzi, Jr.	CFR
Franklin Williams	CFR
John D. Wilson	CFR

BANKERS TRUST CO.

Alfred Brittain, III	CFR
David O. Beim	CFR
Carlos Canal, Jr.	CFR
Richard L. Gelb	CFR
Calvin H. Plimpton	CFR
Patricia Stewart	CFR
John W. Brooks	CFR
Vernon Jordon, Jr.	CFR
Wm. Tavoulareas	CFR

MORGAN GUARANTY

Lewis T. Preston	CFR
Alex. Vagliano	CFR
Rimmer deVries	CFR
Jackson B. Gilbert	CFR
Ray C. Adam	CFR
Carter L. Burgess	CFR
Frank T. Cary	CFR
Emilio G. Collado	CFR
Alan Greenspan	CFR
Howard Johnson	CFR
James L. Ketelsen	CFR
Walter H. Page	CFR
Ellmore Patterson	CFR
J. Paul Austin	TC

CHEMICAL BANK

Donald C. Platten	CFR
Charles Carson, Jr.	CFR
Richard LeBlond, II	CFR
Walter V. Shipley	CFR
Robert J. Callander	CFR
Frederick L. Deming	CFR

1st NATL. OF CHICAGO

Wm. McDonough	CFR
Robert S. Ingersoll	CFR TC
Brooks McCormick	CFR
Lee L. Morgan	CFR

MANUFACTURERS HANOVER

Charles J. Pilliod, Jr.	CFR

The "NEW WORLD ORDER" views of Rockefeller, Kissinger, Brzezinski and others in the CFR/TC "inner circle" are not shared by all members. Some join for prestige and to further their careers. Some are invited in for "window dressing". All Americans should closely examine the disastrous results of foreign and domestic policy formulated and implemented by the CFR through the years without public knowledge.

MEDIA
Past & Present CFR/TC Members (partial listing)

CBS
William Paley	CFR
William Burden	CFR
Roswell Gilpatric	CFR
Henry Schacht	CFR TC
Marietta Tree	CFR
C.C. Collingwood	CFR
Lawrence LeSueur	CFR
Dan Rather	CFR
Harry Reasoner	CFR
Richard Hottelet	CFR
Frank Stanton	CFR
Bill Moyer	CFR

NBC/RCA
Jane Pfeiffer	CFR
Lester Crystal	CFR
R.W. Sonnenfeldt	CFR
T.F. Bradshaw	CFR
John Petty	CFR
David Brinkley	CFR
John Chancellor	CFR
Marvin Kalb	CFR
Irvine Levine	CFR
P.G. Peterson	CFR TC
John Sawhill	CFR TC

ABC
Ray Adam	CFR
Frank Cary	CFR
T.M. Macioce	CFR
Ted Koppel	CFR
John Scali	CFR
Barbara Walters	CFR

CABLE NEWS NETWORK
Daniel Schorr	CFR

PUBLIC BROADCAST SERVICE
Hartford Gunn	CFR
Robert McNeil	CFR
Jim Lehrer	CFR
C. Hunter-Gault	CFR
Hodding Carter	CFR

ASSOCIATED PRESS
Keith Fuller	CFR
Stanley Swinton	CFR
Louis Boccardi	CFR
Harold Anderson	CFR

U.P.I.
H.L. Stevenson	CFR

REUTERS
Michael Posner	CFR

BOSTON GLOBE
David Rogers	CFR

L.A. TIMES SYNDICATE
Tom Johnson, Jr.	TC
Joseph Kraft	CFR TC

BALTIMORE SUN
Henry Trewhitt	CFR

CHICAGO SUN TIMES
James Hoge	CFR TC

MINNEAPOLIS STAR/TRIBUNE
John Cowles, Jr.	CFR TC

HOUSTON POST
William P. Hobby	CFR

NEW YORK TIMES CO.
Richard Gelb	CFR
James Reston	CFR
William Scranton	CFR TC
A.M. Rosenthal	CFR
Seymour Topping	CFR
James Greenfield	CFR
Max Frankel	CFR
Jack Rosenthal	CFR
Harding Bancroft	CFR
Amory Bradford	CFR
Orvil Dryfoos	CFR
David Halberstram	CFR
Walter Lippmann	CFR
L.E. Markel	CFR
H.L. Matthews	CFR
John Oakes	CFR
Adolph Ochs	CFR
Harrison Salisbury	CFR
A. Hays Sulzberger	CFR
A. Ochs Sulzberger	CFR
C.L. Sulzberger	CFR
H.L. Smith	CFR
Steven Rattner	CFR
Richard Burt	CFR

TIME INC.
Ralph Davidson	CFR
Donald M. Wilson	CFR
Louis Banks	CFR
Henry Grunwald	CFR
Alexander Heard	CFR
Sol Linowitz	CFR TC
Rawleigh Warner, Jr.	CFR
Thomas Watson, Jr.	CFR

NEWSWEEK/WASH. POST
Katharine Graham	CFR
Philip Graham	CFR
Arjay Miller	TC
N. deB. Katzenbach	CFR
Frederick Beebe	CFR
Robert Christopher	CFR
A. De Borchgrave	CFR
Osborne Elliot	CFR
Philip Geyelin	CFR
Kermit Lausner	CFR
Murry Marder	CFR
Eugene Meyer	CFR
Malcolm Muir	CFR
Maynard Parker	CFR
George Will	CFR
Robert Kaiser	CFR
Meg Greenfield	CFR
Walter Pincus	CFR
Murray Gart	CFR
Peter Osnos	CFR
Don Oberdorfer	CFR

DOW JONES & CO.
(Wall St. Journal)
William Agee	CFR
J. Paul Austin	TC
Charles Meyer	CFR
Robert Potter	CFR
Richard Wood	CFR
Robert Bartley	CFR
Karen House	CFR

NATIONAL REVIEW
Wm. F. Buckley, Jr.	CFR
Richard Brookhiser	CFR

BRUCE BABBITT
CFR   TC
ADV. COMMISSION ON INTERGOVERNMENTAL RELATIONS

ROBERT ANDERSON
CFR
DEPT. OF LABOR

William Brock, Jr. CFR TC
(Special Trade Rep.)
Eleanor Norton CFR
(Nat'l Comm. for Employment Policy)

UNION BOSSES

I.W. Abel (Former President, United Steelworkers of America)   TC

Sol Chick Chaikin (President, Int. Ladies' Garment Workers)   CFR TC

Thomas R. Donahue (Secretary/Treasurer, AFL-CIO)   CFR TC

Murray H. Finley (President, Amalgamated Clothing & Textile Workers)   CFR

Victor Gotbaum   CFR
(American Fed. of State, County and Municipal Employees)

Lane Kirkland (Pres. AFL-CIO)   CFR TC

Howard D. Samuel (President, Industrial Union Dept. AFL-CIO)   CFR

Martin J. Ward (President, United Assn. of Journeymen and Apprentices of the Plumbing and Pipe Fitting Industry, U.S.A. & Canada)   CFR TC

Glenn E. Watts (President, Communications Workers of America)   CFR TC

Leonard Woodcock   CFR TC
(Former President U.A.W.)

Jerry Wurf (President, American Federation of State, County and Municipal Employees)   CFR

PLEASE DISTRIBUTE WIDELY

WRITE FOR THIS
❖❖❖ INFORMATION ❖❖❖

* REAGAN and CARTER charts.
* Analysis of CFR/TC & members listing.
* The NEW WORLD ORDER explained.
* Analysis of Federal Reserve fraud (inflation + excessive interest rates = depression and foreclosures.)
* The Media Propaganda machine.
* CFR Military control = no-win wars.
* The attack on Christian schools.

Send $5.00 postage/handling to:
Johnny Stewart
F.R.E.E.
1807 Columbus Avenue
Box 8616 • Waco, Texas 76710
(817) 756-6831

CHAPTER 3

Congressional Elections

We would like to think of our Congress as being composed of patriotic, dedicated men who offered themselves and their time in service of their country. Although some start with such high purposes, few retain them. The Congressional election system rules out such fanciful ideas.

The Spoils System
As Seen From Within

Charles A. Lindbergh, father of the flyer, as Congressman, fought the passage of the Federal Reserve Act of 1913. Still in Congress in the early twenties, he wrote the following:

"Politics have been controlled by a trick; the decoy has been to hold up beautiful and true principles for honest action . . . the same ideals stated in different words are advanced by the other party. When the election is over, the capitalists control. . . .

"Office holders," Congressman Lindbergh said, "understand that by joining with the interest to exploit the people, their reelection is more certain than if they serve the people who elect them. . . . If the electorate should get Congress to introduce a bill for reform, the writing of that bill would be turned over to profiteers and the bill, when written, would carry the reform's name, but would frequently make things worse.

"Should a Congressman introduce reform bills, the bills are sure to have first been gone over by the profiteers' lobbyists. They are on their guard for their clients at all times and investigate everything. Should such a bill run the gauntlet and get on the floor, all sorts of wiles, rules and tricks would be used by Congress to defeat it and to keep the public from finding out how each legislator voted."

At the Present

It costs money to be elected to Congress. Money is needed to organize the campaign, for aides, stenographers, postage, telephone calls, travel, newspaper advertisements and for television coverage. (It has been stated that a 30-second prime-time television spot in a city the size of St. Louis may cost as much as $10,000.) According to the Federal Election Commission the 1982 Congressional election cost $344 million.

Some people interested in a candidate's general qualifications and philosophy give small amounts — usually in answer to requests. A few seats are won by very wealthy candidates — at the cost of a million dollars of personal money.

Then there are the loners looking for profit:

"Billionaire's Business Is Political," was a headline over a full page spread in *The Charlotte Observer,* on December 21, 1975. It was said of Howard Hughes, but is true of almost all very wealthy men. It is the way they became very wealthy. In the same issue an article by Donald L. Bartlett and James A. Steele tells of Hughes' contributions to public officials; of intrigue and quiet understandings; of cash flow to Hughes of $6 billion in ten years; of the fact that the Civil Aeronautics Board, Internal Revenue Service and the courts shielded him from rules and regulations of law.

The legal limit for private contributions is $1,000 for each election.

Much of the money comes from secret slush funds — the buying of candidates and their official actions by special interest groups. And then there are the Political Action Committees, called PACS.

These committees were started by labor unions in 1940, to raise voluntary funds from union members to give to candidates favoring unions. At that time the Hatch Act forbade corporations from collecting such funds. The 1974 Fair Campaign Practice Act revoked the Hatch Act. Two years later the Supreme Court ruled that if there is no communication between giver and candidate, the amount spent in his behalf is unlimited. (Is this the Court's idea of the meaning of the constitutional guarantee of free speech?)

Since then Political Action Committees have spread through industry and through the nation. There are today 3371 of these committees. Each of these committees may give a candidate $5,000 in the primary, and $10,000 in the election. In 1982 these committees gave candidates $83 million.

(Some candidates do not spend all donated money in their campaigns, but keep and make personal use of the remainder. Some buy expensive cars; some, jewelry for their wives; some take trips abroad.)

Some of these committees are organized to defeat the re-election of congressmen who have not gone along with them.

Contributions from the very wealthy and from Political Action committees are not always given with the idea of good government in mind. They are given for some specific favored treatment. This may not be mentioned, but the implication is there, and they get it.

Other groups raise their voices — the feminists, ethnic groups, and the "gay rights" crowd. "Vote our way or we will beat you at the polls." Seldom is there a selfless call for all factions to forego favored treatment and render all possible aid for the good of all.

Congressional Aides

Congressmen are kept busy attending sessions, committee meetings, seeing constituents and trying to get reelected. They have little time to read and understand the page after page of jargon in the hundreds of bills brought before Congress each year. They employ aides to assist them, now almost 19,000 in all.

These aides advise congressmen as to how to vote. They may stand by him to coach when the bill comes up for debate. Their influence is very great. They have been called the "shadow government."

When lobbyists want some special bill for the privilege of their employer, they go first to the aides. These may or may not oblige. In one case an aide inserted a million-dollar deduction into a tax exempt bill, after it had been passed into law. (This was discovered and removed.)

The tenure of office for aides is at the pleasure of the congressman employing them. If the congressman is defeated at the polls, the aides with him are out of a job. Some may go to other congressmen. Some may go to higher government office. Some who have pleased lobbyists are given lucrative jobs in the private sector.

Lobbyists

Once a legislator is elected, lobbyists gather about the new official. Banks offer bargain loans. There are tips on good buys in the stock market.

"Much is at stake in the public policy that will be made by office holders — who will pay most of the taxes in an increasingly expensive welfare-warfare state, who will get contracts of $100 million, $500 million, $1 billion, where the $200-million roads and dams will go and where they won't go."

As far back as February 21, 1976, Jack Anderson said: "Lobbyists literally swarm over Capitol Hill, hobnob with military brass of the Pentagon, and pull strings inside the White House." They have steadily increased in number. There are now some 6,500 registered lobbyists. It is believed that there are at least 15,000. Lobbyists handle most of the millions of dollars of the PACS. They make friends of important officials, perform every possible favor, pass money to them, "to help with your campaign," all to gain special privileges for their employers. Some representatives who would not accept an envelope of money, see no wrong in accepting fees from their law office back home — employed by some great corporation. Other congressmen, for a sizable fee, deliver lectures, chiefly to officials of companies and organizations having an interest in their vote.

Once such money is accepted; once a politician considers these contributors his chief constituents; once he compromises his vote, there is a breach of character. From then on the taking of money comes easily and so does the betrayal.

The Afterglow

While in office many, perhaps most, officials prepare for their future by handing out favors. Defeated, they do not fade away. They know the ropes. They know those who hand out contracts; those who make the laws. As lobbyists and liaison agents they can get favors and money from the government. For this service corporations pay them more money than they ever made.

The *U.S. News & World Report* (9/7/81): "Last year alone, more than a third of the Senators and House members who quit or lost at the polls were employed by Washington-based special-interest groups, corporations and law firms."

And again, in its December 7, 1981, issue:

"How Carter Crew Is Cashing In After Defeat
"A survey indicates that the 1981 earnings of Carter's top White House and Cabinet officials will average above $300,000. Said former Commerce Secretary Juanita Kreps, who sits as director on seven corporate boards: 'I know how the government works.' "

The Way Our Government Works

In a Congressional Committee hearing on a $98.3-billion tax increase, and an attempted $17-billion saving on the 1983 budget, held August 5-15, 1982, the possibility of saving by a cut on the Medicare appropriation came up.

It was shown that a heart pacemaker, costing $700 to produce, was sold to hospitals for $5,000, and more to patients; that doctors were charging exorbitant fees for their simple placement and after-care; that there were kickbacks to some, perhaps many doctors and hospital officials; that 100 pacemaker salesmen were making $200,000 a year in salaries and commissions; a dozen, $1 million; that 30 to 50 percent of placements were unnecessary, and that Medicare is paying 80 to 85 percent of the bill.

The American Medical Association was looking after

doctors' interests in this and also in other topics on the agenda. Its *NEWS* of August 27, 1982, stated that their lobbyists and some hundred others stayed with the Committee until 4 a.m. Said Michael Bromberg, executive director of American Hospitals: "As always, the AMA people were always there, were seen everywhere, did a wonderful job and came out better than anyone."

Our most important legislation is conducted in such an atmosphere.

The *U.S. News & World Report* (9/19/83) stated that at one tax hearing there were so many lobbyists that they could not get into the hearing room. "The hallway was so filled with smoke that you could hardly see from one end to the other."

Many lobbyists are experts in their line. Congressmen depend upon them for advice. This advice is always slanted to the interests of those who employ them.

Foreign Lobbies

Of all the congressmen who were approached in Abscam, only one refused the money.

Foreign lobbies are big business. All of their expenses are borne by American citizens — directly or indirectly. Their detrimental influence is very great.

In the fall of 1976 it was disclosed that in foregoing years Korea's President Park had sent agents with expensive gifts and millions of dollars (of our taxpayers' money) to influence Washington officials to countenance his oppressions, and to send him more money. Ninety congressmen were under investigation in this scandal. Park said he would be a witness. He did not live to tell the story. The investigation quieted down.

In lobbying for free trade Japan employed Frank Church,

former U.S. Senate Foreign Relations Chairman, former Cabinet officials, and other former congressmen and prominent lawyers — some 80 in all. Their job is to influence lawmakers, and clear the way for the selling of billions more in goods in the United States than we sell to Japan.

Said Representative Rosenthal (D-NY): "Foreign powers are able to hire very distinguished Americans with fine records to do their bidding, frequently when these interests are contrary to American interest" (*U.S. News & World Report,* 3/29/82). The article names former Cabinet members, senators, representatives and other officials — even former President Ford.

Congressmen tell us that receiving favors and money does not influence their votes. This is simply not true. Special interest groups would not spend the large amounts of money if this did not bring results. It is hard to vote against a man who has given you several thousand dollars.

A number of times tallies have been taken of Congressional votes on some bill, cast before and after congressmen received money from the bill's sponsor. The shift from "no" to "yes" tells the story.

The *U.S. News & World Report* (2/23/81) quotes Representative Thomas J. Downey (D-NY) as saying: "The lobbying process is fueled by campaign contributions. The correlation between contributions and votes is remarkable."

To repay their obligations, and in hopes of more, congressmen give their great contributors everything they ask for. The business of catering to them overrides all other concerns.

An action requested by a lobbyist may appear as an amendment, perhaps unprinted, which may change, pass or defeat some bill. A requested bill may be locked, as a rider, to an unrelated bill in the last stages of legislative action. Or again, it may be brought up when only a few lawmakers are present, and passed by a show of hands rather than by a recorded voice vote.

Those who would know more about this should read an article by John A. Long and Robert A. Barr in the *U.S. News & World Report* (7/19/82), "Legalized Bribery." Said Representative Tobby Moffett (D-CT): "One can envision a situation where we have some members of Congress being virtually on retainer to the major corporations of this country." Said Representative Patricia Schroder (D-CO), "We are becoming the finest Congress money can buy."

A Recent Appraisal

U.S. News & World Report (1/9/84) gives the view of Congress as expressed by 120 former members. It may be summed up in a quotation from Hamer Budge, Republican House member from Idaho 1951-1961:

"Congress is ceasing to be a group of representative citizens chosen from many walks of life and is becoming a self-perpetuating collection of professional politicians or bureaucrats sustained by special interest groups or organizations."

The Congressional Record

I used to go to the public library to read the *Congressional Record:* to see exactly what some congressman said about some bill. I stopped going for this when I found that I could not tell fact from fiction.

Since then I have read several articles telling of the falsification of this supposedly open, honest publication. A recent one is in *Reader's Digest* (February, 1983): "Congress's License to Lie," by James Nathan Miller. Mr. Miller tells that the *Congressional Record* speeches are changed, added, or withdrawn, that: " . . . up to 70 percent of what's in it was never spoken on the floor, and 10 to 15 percent of what's spoken doesn't get in it."

The Bureaucrats

Following the enactment of a law, the related subdivision of the executive branch must interpret and enforce it.

The plain wording of the law, supported by the usual laws of fraud and laws of equity, should be enough. Instead, bureaus come into the picture. These bureaus qualify for the definition for them given in *Webster's New Collegiate Dictionary:* "A system of administration marked by officialism, red tape and proliferation." Into these bureaus, on government payroll, politicians place their relatives, friends and contributors. There are also career bureaucrats, more powerful than politicians, the "Civil Service Establishment."

Many articles have been written on this subject. A good one is to be found in *Reader's Digest,* June, 1979. Professor Murray S. Weidenbaum states that in this field some 55 Federal agencies employ some 80 thousand people.

Rather than sit idle, these bureaucrats complicate and compound the simplest laws. Rulings of the Occupational, Safety and Health Administration fill a stack of books more than twelve feet high. Paul Harvey read one of these rules: "Safety glasses shall be worn when applying or removing these articles." It was on a box of thumb tacks.

The Editor's Page of *U.S. News & World Report* (10/30/79) stated that a small business man has to plow through 70,000 pages of Federal regulations every twelve months; that a man owning a moderate-sized filling station said he spent 610 hours a year completing Federal, State and County forms.

The cost of these regulations is put at $1 billion a year. The total damage to society and our freedom is very great.

Sidelines

Congress provides "assistance" to the little man.

Actions at this level amount to practically nothing in the overall scheme. As we shall presently see, all actions, all favors here are but a part of the financiers' grand scheme. Financiers, like sharks, are swallowing big fish intent on swallowing little ones.

One example tells the story:

Because of the farmers' lobby and because of the farmers' votes, the government lends money to the farmer and provides crop subsidies. At the same time the government is, through a higher lobby, helping the bankers take his farm. The money the government loans to the farmer is borrowed at high interest from bankers. This enriches the bankers; and payment of interest by the farmer along with higher taxes make up the difference in interest between that charged the government and that the government charges the farmer. This is a severe drain on the farmer. The government allows great financiers to monopolize the manufacture of farm machinery and sell at exorbitant prices. A grain combine belt which should sell at a few dollars is replaced with another one priced at $110. The government gives the nation's oil to the bankers' great oil companies, and deregulating the price of oil allows these oil companies to sell oil to farmers at ruinous prices. The government, bowing to labor unions' lobbyists, forces the farmer to pay the high minimum wage to laborers. The government allows great bankers to buy up the seed companies, patent seed and charge exorbitant prices for it. Fertilizer and everything else the farmer buys is priced to him. The great grain companies, subsidized by the government, price the farmer's grain. Great corporate farms get most of the farm subsidy.

In the end the government sells the family-owned farmer's machinery and farm at auction.

CHAPTER 4

Charters, Corporations and Mergers

To refresh my memory and get exact dictionary meanings, I look up almost every word. Here, the meaning of two words are so important that I repeat their definitions to you.

A charter is defined as a grant of privilege from the sovereign power of a state or country — in this case, a writ of incorporation.

A corporation is an artificial person, created by law from a group of natural persons having a continuous existence and powers and liabilities distinct from those of its members.

A corporation is simply this and nothing more. A state or country gets nothing for granting this privilege.

Corporations are necessary in our system of free enterprise, but the power of corporations should be limited by the definition of free enterprise. This is, to repeat, the freedom of private business to organize and operate for profit in a competitive system, without interference by government beyond regulation necessary to protect private interest and keep the national economy in balance.

Constitutional prerogatives reserved for the government and constitutional safeguards designed for protection of the individual are now claimed by corporations. These soulless corporations, having been given individual rights by law, now ride roughshod over the living. Many of today's corporations are bogus, or dummy ones, created for the purpose of concealment and extortion. Many, through bribery of our officials, have bilked our government out of all profit from control of our money, and out of our natural resources. They have now gained monopolies on almost all of the necessities of life.

They have opened great supermarket chains that sell almost everything, and perform many services — denying opportunity to others. They employ executives and lobbyists to think up ways and laws to strip the people and the nation of all wealth. They have laws passed to permit them to create great unlimited corporations, and to merge these into great combines.

As long as giant corporations hold their present charters and are allowed to secrete their holdings by layer upon layer of subsidiary charters, the public is helpless before them.

Their directors are so interlocked, their ways so secret and so devious, their records so often falsified, and their system of bookkeeping so bewildering, that no outsider can see beneath the surface. No government examiner can say whether this corporation, or that, owes taxes. No commissioner, even if completely selfless, can know the validity of their incessant demands for more.

An example of secrecy and lack of control is seen in Florida. Under the laws any person or any corporation can charter a corporation in secrecy. A single attorney enjoying attorney-client immunity, can be named as every officer of the corporation. Over 181,700 active corporations are registered in the state of Florida — up 36,672 in one single year.

Such secrecy, without the knowledge of our State Department, allows foreign citizens and foreign governments to operate within the United States in peace or in war with all that portends. Such secrecy allows criminals to engage in legitimate business. It permits corporations of good repute to cover up their holdings and avoid responsibility for their actions.

Many corporations hold charters of such wide scope and of such diversity that they restrain manufacture and trade. Huge corporations are permitted to use their enormous wealth to contend for profit in any area, and in almost any sideline.

It is one thing to permit a man to operate a very large store. It is quite another to allow great corporations to establish chain stores all over the nation to sell almost every type of goods and services. Such a course denies opportunity to others.

It is one thing to charter and permit a company to engage in the production of oil, another company to run a railroad, another company to operate a bank; and quite another thing to allow a corporation to do all of these and to also operate farms, denying opportunity to individuals, families, and smaller operations.

The handful of men who own great corporations control our government and hold this nation and its people in their hands.

Monopoly

Monopoly is the very antithesis of free enterprise. It implies the exclusive control of public service, or exclusive power to buy and/or sell a commodity in a specified area. Monopoly is gained through legal privileges, command of supplies, threats, or force. Monopoly plays its deadening role in most transactions in this nation, even the smaller ones.

The Merger

The third great merger wave of the century is now surging through the ranks of American corporations.

Some mergers have been happy ones. Many have aroused bitterness among the stockholders, and consternation among ousted executives and replaced employees.

Great banks supply the money for many of these mergers, and either enter into the business or else divide the spoils.

A detailed and enlightening account of the merger is given by James Boyd in *Men of Distinction.* Mr. Boyd states that involuntary mergers are effected by spying, bribery of trusted officials, and false reports to stockholders who are required to pay for false appraisals. Often the surrounded company is looted of its assets. This important exposé is must reading.

Conglomerates continue to grow. Some list hundreds of great companies. Their incomes are greater than most nations. They stifle competition and independent action in America and extend their tentacles to the farthest reaches of the earth. They enlist the services of the United States government to overthrow governments of small nations opposing them — or to placate the government of great countries in which they wish to operate.

The *Christian Science Monitor* (3/16/81) stated that within one week there were three separate billion-dollar mergers, mostly by oil companies — flush with profits from the decontrol of oil prices — as they bought Kennicott Copper and other rich mineral companies.

Mergers continue. From time to time lists of mergers are published. A report in *U.S. News & World Report* (3/26/84) names ten mergers involving $66 billion or more.

On August 5, 1981, the DuPont-Conoco merger was announced. This involved more than $7 billion.

Exxon has bought Reliance Electric Company which has

sales of some billion dollars a year.

Oil companies with their enormous profits are not so much interested in digging new wells as they are in buying other companies which have wells. All through December 1981 we read of Mobil Oil's determined effort to swallow Marathon Oil Company. It offered $6.5 billion. One day after winning a temporary ban on the competing U.S. Steel's bid, it threatened to take over U.S. Steel Company.

The Library of Congress has determined that total mergers for 1981 were $82.6 billion.

In January of 1984, Texaco announced its agreement with Getty Oil to buy the latter company for $9.9 billion, the largest corporate merger in U.S. history, unless the government approved Standard Oil of California's bid for Gulf Oil Corporation for $13.4 billion.

How does it happen that all these financiers have billions of dollars, like so much pocket change, and the rest of us have practically nothing, and that mortgaged to them? As Ernest Ross says, in *The Freeman Digest* (December 1983), "One cannot initiate new economic action when nearly every field of endeavor is locked up and coercively protected for the politically favored and powerful."

As mergers get larger, monopolies are concentrated into fewer hands. Smaller businesses cannot operate, and 26,000 firms had reported bankruptcy for the year as of December 1, 1983.

CHAPTER 5

Monopoly on Food

The Russian Wheat Deal

Through the years the financiers, interested in profits from food, drew concession after concession from the government, and added shopping centers to their holdings. A near monopoly had been achieved. Still the price of food remained comparatively low. There was a huge reserve, a government stockpile of grain, paid for by, and belonging to, all the people. There was also a great deal of grain in dealers' elevators. Such an abundance guaranteed food for the nation and tended to hold prices down.

Then all was changed. The Russians dropped a hint that they were in the market for grain. They refused to say how much grain they had. "There is a law against telling," they said. Those who direct the great American food corporations saw an opportunity for profits. Also, they must have realized that once the nation's grain reserve was swept away, they could charge what they pleased for food. There was secret consultation between government officials and those of food corporations.

Like passing through a revolving door, there was an exchange of government officials and corporate officials. Secretary of Agriculture Hardin was offered and accepted a high position in the Ralston Purina Food Corporation, and Earl Butz, a director of Ralston Purina, took his place as Secretary of Agriculture. On July 8, 1972, it was announced that the United States had sold almost 17 million tons of grain to Russia.

President Nixon approved the sale. Others immediately involved with Secretary Butz were Assistant Secretary of Agriculture Clarence Palmby, who then resigned to become vice president of the Consolidated Grain Company; and U.S. Commodity Credit Corporation's vice president, Clifford Pulvermaster, who also resigned to join a large grain trading company.

Those in on the secret, and the great grain companies, made large profits. For one thing, an immediate subsidy of $300 million was paid by the United States Treasury. Congressman Charles Vanik (D-Ohio) said the deal would cost the United States public $1.5 billion in wheat subsidy and land bank support.

The official reason given for the wheat sale was that it helped balance foreign trade and helped stabilize the dollar. If it did, it was on paper only. The Russians were granted a $750 million credit at 6-1/8 percent interest. All improvement in foreign trade was promptly thrown away by loans to the Russians, and handouts to assist American capitalists to build plants in that country. Billions of dollars of Russia's war debt were canceled and the remainder settled for what proved to be three cents on the dollar — to be paid in the distant future.

In 1973 seven million additional tons of grain were sold to Russia. After America's reserve of grain was cleared away, wheat (sold to Russia for $1.53-$1.56 a bushel) reached $6.30 a bushel in Chicago. In the chain reaction that followed, and in the claims of shortage, the price of food rose sharply. Housewives in the supermarkets stood dismayed as day after day packages of food were stamped higher and higher.

The great corporations had achieved their aim: the control of the price of food.

Our Grain Should Be Kept

The United States continues to deplete its topsoil and water, more precious than oil (which should be husbanded for future generations), to supply food for those who constantly raise the price of their oil in an effort to ruin us financially; and also to feed our deadly enemy who, parading their rockets and stamping soldiers in the streets, declare their determination to bury us.

In his report to Congress the spring of 1982, John Leyman, Secretary of the Navy, stated that the Soviets were engaged in a massive buildup of fleets of airplanes, rockets and other weapons in Cuba, Guyana, and Nicaragua.

Her largest submarines prowl the Caribbean.

To protect her people, Russia has built 15,000 bomb shelters. Some of these are regular cities. All are built against the day when it plans, with rockets, to knock out our missiles; with submarines to cut off our import of oil; and with well-directed shots to destroy our bridges and road centers, bringing all movement of food to a halt.

The Russians are intelligent enough to buy our grain to deplete us, whether they need it or not. They can store it, give it to Cuba and other dependents.

For all the fanfare and money handed out by officials who sit in our Civil Defense offices, the program has made no real move to protect anyone except the Washington politicians, and the Federal Reserve officials — with taxpayer money.

Harrison Horn, in *Spotlight,* tells of a luxurious underground, supposedly bomb-proof shelter at Mt. Pony, Virginia. It was built to protect the personnel and families of the Federal Reserve. It will house 540 people along with the communication system and a large amount of money.

There are reports of enormous caves filled with computer tapes. Other retreats have been built for politicians.

In case of an airstrike we, the people, are to be herded out into the country. What will happen when we need a drink of water, when dinner time comes? The people of this nation could be starved into submission in a few days' time. What about the next crop, and the next?

In January 1981, then Secretary of Agriculture Bergland reported: "Our stockpile of most commodities is dangerously low. The thin margin between security and surplus is more than ever a function of the weather over which we have little control."

We have had a bumper crop since then. We have sold millions of tons of it to foreigners. In September 1982, it was estimated that there was enough unsold grain to feed the nation for 150 days. In case of war and its destruction, it may be years before another crop.

The grain should be kept. Bins and methods for grinding should be built throughout the nation and the grain allotted to them. There should be warnings, encouragements by descriptive publications and tax credits to get people to build their own shelters, and to provision them.

The Takeover of Farms

Our change from an agrarian to an industrial nation was not as voluntary and as gentle as the words might imply.

The nation's monetary system, with its cyclic depressions, forced many a family from the farm and into virtual slavery at the cotton mill or garment sweatshop of some eighty or ninety years ago.

Those who owned the great banks began to see the future harvest and began to collect farms. Then came the dust-bowl years. Steinbeck's *Grapes of Wrath* describes the odyssey of one dispossessed family. The book tells how the bankers took over farm after farm, bulldozed down houses, and heartlessly drove the people from the land. Reaching California this family found most of the groves and cropland already under control of the financiers. Hungry, on the verge of starvation, these penniless people saw great piles of food that could not be sold at a profit, burned — while guards and police stood by with clubs.

The Agriculture Adjustment Act of 1933 implemented a well-planned publically announced policy by the federal government to drive farm families from the soil. The effective device was paying for not planting. Millions of acres were idled. The money, all profit, bought machinery, and millions of sharecroppers were forced from farms.

The great depression hastened the takeover. As long ago as 1935 the largest farmer in California was the Bank of America's California Lands, Inc. It then owned 2,670 farms with a total of 531,000 acres. At that time the bank held mortgages covering 7,398 farms, totalling over a million acres. The increase in the years since then must be enormous.

"The farmers borrowed the money," we are told. Yes, they did. They could not create the money they had to have, but the bankers could, and through this special privilege, the banks took their property.

Farmers have always been our finest citizens. Once they were prosperous in their small way. All but destroyed by a multitude of government regulations, they have now met another threat. Great corporations, operating in other fields, searching for more profit, saw the farmers' land, and wanted it and any profit from it. These corporations, with their enormous wealth, control all markets and prices. They are allowed to compete with and crush every small individual farmer.

The small farmer in moderate circumstances cannot afford to employ untrained laborers and meet their demands for the minimum wage scale; to provide funds for the various insurances, the unemployment reserves; health and safety requirements; environment preservation, rules on employment advances and discharges; tax collections and deductions, social security and the like. Nor can he afford the bookkeeping and time for endless reports.

The small farmer must borrow money to put in his crop.

Great corporations set high prices on farm machinery and spare parts, on gasoline and oil, fertilizer, chemicals, and now, seeds.

No matter how intelligent he is, no matter how hard he works, the small farmer falls behind. If he has a good year he is forced to sell at the price the great corporations dictate. There is never any real security. A bad crop year puts him in perpetual debt — at high interest. Two or three bad years in succession breaks him, and puts him, our finest citizen, in some precarious job or on welfare.

(It is well to mention the fact that no act of God or man ever affects the date or validity of a banker's note. Drought or flood are all the same here; depression with scarcity of money, fire, sickness or death — any of these things affect the borrower's ability to pay. None affect the banker's claim.)

There are continuing reports of farmers forced from their homes, too many to be recorded here.

Flesh and Blood

There were touching scenes on an NBC newscast, March 22, 1982. It showed auction after auction of farm machinery in one county in Georgia. It showed the old farmers who had tilled their land all their lives. It showed the despair, the sorrow, and in some cases, the bitterness.

One farmer's sign read: "They took our gold, they took our silver, they took our grain, and now they want our land."

"Hard Times in the Heartland" *(U.S. News & World Report,* 4/12/82) told how high interest was breaking farmer after farmer. Farmland that sold for $1,200 per acre the year before, now sold for $700. At some auctions there was not a single bid.

And so on through these disastrous years.

At the sale of a farm at Springfield, Colorado, some 200 farmers came to try to prevent the sale. The police drove them back with tear gas and clubs. Newscasts showed farmers with streaks of blood on their heads. One farmer was down with heavy streaks and splotches of blood on his head and chest. The sheriff had a bloody nose. One farmer was arrested. He jumped from a window. Friends cut his handcuff chain.

At the sale of these farms larger farmers or great corporations outbid family farmers and add to their holdings.

With suppression of small farmers, the large corporations have a free hand. They can well afford to employ experts to keep records and reports — slanted in their favor. The expense of all this and any added levy, as well as the taxes, are added to the price of the final product, or declared as a tax loss to offset other, profitable endeavors.

If there is loss on a particular farm, the company does not feel it. They can afford to bide their time. The independent farmer cannot.

The Bankers' Bid to Take Over the Nation's Farms

The following is quoted from an article by Dan McCurry. It was written January 22, 1977.

"On Christmas Day I was down at the *Washington Post* when a UPI story caught my eye:

> 'The Continental Illinois National Bank and Merrill, Lynch, Pierce, Fenner and Smith, Inc., are pleased to announce plans for a pooled agricultural land investment fund. It is the intention of this seventh largest bank in the nation to use the pension fund it holds in trust for workers' retirement to buy $50 million of prime agricultural land. . . .'

Continental Illinois Bank knows how to enlarge every tax loophole they can find. For the year 1973, the year the bank began to discuss Ag Land Fund 1, the bank paid not one cent in effective federal income tax." (Their income for that year was $105.8 million.)

In a Congressional committee meeting February 18, 1977, a great northern bank unfolded its plan to buy and amalgamate farms, thousands of acres, to produce the nation's food. The bank would furnish the land, the machinery, seed and fertilizer, and attend to all business. It might rent some land to sharecroppers, the bank said; the rest would furnish many jobs. The bank did not ask if it could do this. It can. The request was that the operation be made tax-free. Several things should be noted here:

1. Only a small number of our citizens now work for themselves. This plan is calculated to further reduce that number. It would, the farmers attending the meeting said, "give the bank such an advantage that they could not compete, that they would be forced to sell and become slaves of the enterprise."

2. It illustrates the fact that the financiers are determined to complete their control of the nation's food. There could be no check on their involved bookkeeping or on the price they could claim for the food raised. There could be no limit to the land they could annex with their profits.

The tax-free operation was denied.

Yet this rebuff has not fazed the bankers.

The Takeover of Farms Continues

Minerals of the Southern California valleys have not been leached out by rain. The soil is very fertile. There is a lack of rain. To assist the small farmer the government irrigated this land without charge. One of these 320-acre irrigated farms makes more money than 95 percent of all the farms in the United States. A federal law supposedly reserves federal, subsidized irrigation projects for resident, moderate-sized farms. Great corporations have evaded this law. BOSWELL (tied to Los Angeles Times-Mirror Corp.) owns 242 square miles or 155,000 acres; Southern Pacific Railroad 120,000 acres; Tenneco 115,000 acres; Standard Oil (Chevron) 30,000 acres; Los Angeles Times (Te. Ranch) 20,000 acres; Bangor-Punta 38,000 acres; Getty Oil 30,000 acres; Irvine Ranch 88,000 acres; Telles 30,000 acres; Superior Oil 35,000 acres; and so on. The courts have declared this illegal, and now these corporations are attempting to get Congress to make their control of 94 percent of subsidized water perpetual. The government subsidizes about ten million acres.

The Prulene farm in North Carolina consists of 83,000 acres. It is owned by McLean Trucking Company and Prudential Life Insurance Company. Prudential owns more than 750,000 acres of farmland in 16 states. Other insurance companies have bought tens of thousands of acres of farmland. Wall Street brokers are recommending farms as investments.

Coca Cola, through its subsidiary, Minute Maid, owns some 85,000 acres of Florida orange groves. It also owns large groves in California. Purex and United Brands raise a large part of the nation's vegetables. Purina raises the chickens.

Grain

In his *Merchants of Grain,* Dan Morgan states that five great companies: Cargill, Continental, Louis Dreyfus, Bunge, and André, owned by seven of the world's richest families, control the world grain trade.

These companies operate in secret. No one knows their profit, nor how much tax they pay, if any. We do know that the government has subsidized them with many billions of dollars. These companies set the price paid farmers for grain. The prices set will break every independent farmer.

Despite great government surpluses of grain, corporations owning large farms (their land paid for, and their crops put in with money they get for nothing) have made every effort to increase that surplus — forcing out the small farmer. In 1983 the American taxpayers not only paid for their food; they also paid $21.8 billion in farm subsidies. Most of this money will go to big farms — the very ones causing the trouble.

As the conglomerates push for greater, temporary profits, growing far more grain than the nation needs, our natural resources, water and soil, far more precious than money or oil, are being used up at an alarming rate.

Paul Harvey repeated a statement that is now often heard. When the first immigrants came to America, the topsoil depth was 18 inches. It is now eight inches.

Great grain crops are grown on farms of the High Plains from northern Texas to northern Nebraska. This is an arid region of usually light rainfall.

An article in *U.S. News & World Report* (6/29/81) on dropping water tables, especially beneath this land, shows that such natural resources are limited.

"Irrigated-crop acreage in the U.S.," said the news weekly, "has almost tripled in the last three decades, now consuming more than 80% of all the water used in the nation. About 40% of that irrigation comes from underground formations of porous, water-bearing rock known as aquifers."

America's largest such underground lake is the Ogallala Aquifer, beneath the High Plains. It supplies two million people with drinking water. It also irrigates the area which grows 25% of the nation's cotton; 38.5% of the grain sorghum; 16% of the wheat; 13% of the corn; 40% of the grain-fed beef in the final, feed-lot stage. Yet the Ogallala is falling as much as three feet per year in some areas. An engineering expert has said, "We are overdrafting underground water tables by 26%. This means that for every 100 gallons taken out, only 74 are being returned" *(ibid.)*.

The same article also states that the cost of raising this water to the surface has jumped from 18 cents to $2.40 per 1,000 cubic feet in the last decade.

"We'll run out of money before we run out of water," predicted a farmer in New Mexico *(ibid.)*.

Yet, irrigation cost is only *one* of the factors forcing farmers not to raise grain. Another is government coercion, through the lure of monetary reward *not* to grow crops.

For the stated purpose of inducing farmers to plant less, and to reduce the amount of government food in storage, the Agriculture Department created PIK (Payment in Kind) in 1983. This gives farmers who do not plant the amount of farm produce that their land would have brought if it had been cultivated. It is the Agriculture Adjustment Act of 1913, all over again. It will drive small farmers from the land. The program will cost about $12 billion. Most of this will go to great corporations.

Everett Rank, head of Agriculture Service and Stabilization Services, is chief administrator of PIK. From it he and his partners will receive more than $1 million worth of cotton.

The government, controlled by owners of the great corporations, assists in the takeover of farms.

The result of a two-year study by Robert Bergland, the recent Secretary, is published by the United States Department of Agriculture, January 1981, *A Time to Choose.*

The report points out that the people are taxed and forced to pay more for food to provide farm price supports, and as these supports are pegged to the amount of produce sold, most of the money goes to owners of large farms. And further, tax laws, regulations, research, commodity and credit policies, inflation, the marketing system, food processing and distribution and retailing are all biased toward wealthy investors and serve to further concentrate farmlands into their hands.

About 2.7 percent of the people live on farms; less than those own them. In a country where wide ownership of property was a cherished dream! Of these owners about five percent, or some .0015 percent of the population, own 48 percent of the farms and ranch land. About one-third of the farmland is owned by non-farming landlords. There are many farms that have sales of more than $200,000 a year, and 370 of these have sales of over $23 million each.

Mr. Bergland states that: "... unless present policies and programs are changed so that they counter instead of reinforce and accelerate the trend towards ever-larger farming operations, the result will be a few large farms controlling food production in a few years."

Monopoly on Seed

A few decades ago farmers selected, from their cribs, the largest and most perfect ears of corn as seed for their next year's crop. Gardeners raised rare and nutritious vegetables — tender tomatoes that when broken would sparkle in the light, and when eaten, thin skin and all, would reward us with a delightful flavor.

Gardeners saved seed from many plants. For the rest there were seed company catalogues which offered a wide choice at reasonable prices.

Then things began to change. By cross-fertilization of these existing plants, new varieties could easily be produced. Some of these new plants bore fruit that was large and showy, but almost tasteless. Some gave greater yield.

Great multinational corporations, thirsting for profit, saw the possibilities for monopolies on seeds. For some 40 years they fought for a law allowing them to patent and control new plants. They finally won. Late in the evening on the last day Congress met for that year, it passed the Plant Variety Protection Act of 1970.

Corporations here and abroad moved rapidly. They bought up existing seed companies. Their seed catalogues were filled with glowing descriptions of new plants, each followed by the letters VP (variety protected), and at the bottom of the page the warning: "Unauthorized propagation prohibited." Seeds from these new plants are priced higher and higher. According to an unpublished report from the National Science Foundation (using U.S. Dept. of Agriculture data), seed prices have risen faster than any other farm input cost.

By dint of advertising, these corporations have extended their control of seeds throughout the world — in Turkey, in India, in the Orient. In West Germany 95 percent of the seeds offered for sale are protected. In the United Kingdom all cereals are protected. Should an English farmer save and plant such seeds, the authorities would destroy his crop and fine or jail him.

American-based corporations desired more stringent laws here. They also wanted to include some plants not covered. They asked Congress to pass S.23, an amendment to the Variety Protection Act.

At the Senate Agriculture Subcommittee hearing on this amendment, June 17, 1980, Cary Fowler of the Frank P. Graham Center read an informative paper. Most of the following is taken, by permission, from his testimony. I list a few of the corporations which entered this business, and the seed companies they have bought.

New Owner	*Seed Company*
Cargill	Dorman Seeds
	P.A.G.
Celanese	Capril Inc.
	Joseph Harris Seed Co.
	Moran Seeds
I.T.T.	Burpees/O.M. Scott
Purex	Advanced Seeds
	Hulting Hybrids
Union Carbide	Ferry-Morse
	Keystone Seed Co.
Upjohn	Asgrow Seeds
	Associated Seeds

One or two corporations hold 100 percent of the patents on cauliflower and tobacco. Three hold 80 percent of the patents on beans. Four hold 36 to 60 percent of the patents on cotton, lettuce, peas, soybeans and wheat.

Many of these new plants produce fruit lacking in taste. Many are of commercial quality, thick skinned for shipping or for gassing for a red color. Most are of unknown resistance to blight, disease and insects. Blight in the new corn is common. At one time it destroyed 50 percent of the crop in some southern states. The old, traditional corn, standing alongside, was unaffected.

Corporations which hold patents on plants feature these in their catalogues and as rapidly as possible phase out the traditional varieties — capable of reproducing themselves while hybrids are not. Thus wonderful plants, developed by natural and human selection over thousands of years, are lost forever.

There was mounting opposition to the amendment when, suddenly, by a parliamentary maneuver, it was taken from the Committee and brought to the Senate floor. Christmas week, 1980, the lame duck Congress passed Amendments S.23 and H.R.999 extending the Plant Variety Protection Act of 1970, and lame duck President Carter signed them into law.

It was pointed out by Dr. Kenneth Dahlberg that almost all plant development has been done by nature and our ancestors and only one-tenth of one percent by the corporations. He said these corporations should not be allowed a monopoly.

The heart of the discussion — the thought that concerns us here — was stated by bishops of the Catholic Church representing 43 dioceses of 12 midwestern states: "The control of seeds, because it implies also the control of food production and indeed of life itself, should not be appropriated to itself by any company or nation."

Conceivable conditions may arise which would result in the refusal of some of these corporations to supply seeds to some nations: perhaps even this one.

The Processing of Food

Not waiting until they could control all farms, great corporations, seeing opportunity for monopoly and profit, moved to control the processing and sale of food.

Under the caption "Monopolies Boost Food Prices," *The Asheville Citizen* (12/11/73) stated that following a government study the testimony of competent experts is that "Corporate giants dominating the food industry are interested solely in profit and efficiency," and that because of their monopoly, "Consumers pay more, perhaps as much as $3 billion annually, for produce that has less and less nutritional quality and taste."

International corporations have moved rapidly since then. They now own most of the canning and processing plants, the presses that print the colored wrappers, and the supermarkets where final prices are set.

Liberty Lobby's *Spotlight* (2/8/82) painted a grim picture on this subject. It stated that a CIA report in 1980 warned that by 1981, twenty-five huge international corporations would control 74.6 percent of the world's food processing. *Spotlight* went on to state that two megacorporations, Unilever and Brooke-Liebig, control 95 percent of the world's tea supply. Unilever, a vast megacorporation with headquarters in Western Europe, also controls one-third of the world's supply of edible fats and oils. Other multinationals, Cargill, Bunge & Born, CPC and Anderson-Clayton, control most of the other two-thirds.

Eighty-nine percent of fruit production is controlled by United Brands, Standard Fruit, and Del Monte. Three transnational conglomerates, Nestles, Carnation and Kraft, control most processed dairy products.

Four giant meat packers — Swift (a subsidiary of Esmark Corporation), Wilson (a subsidiary of LTV), Armour (owned by Greyhound), Cudahy (General Host) — control more than half of the worldwide beef and pork processing infrastructure. These four are now for sale to a fifth giant — Iowa Beef Processors, controlled by Armond Hammer, chairman of Occidental Petroleum Corporation, and lifetime supporter of the U.S.S.R. *The Spotlight* concludes, "The prospects of supermarket prices, rigged, manipulated and inflated by a global cartel exactly as they raised gas costs, is a threatening one."

The effect of all this is felt everywhere. For most people fine food is a thing of the past. As prices rise most people look for cheaper cuts and accept substitutes. Hot dogs and hamburgers furnish much of our diet.

Housewives read newspapers and clip supermarket coupons in the hope of saving a few cents. They do not need advertisements to help in the selection of good foods, but they are constantly bombarded with them and required to pay for them in every purchase. It is likely that this is the most expensive charge on many foods. (Corn for which farmers received $2.30 a bushel is made into breakfast food, packaged, and sold for $88.55 a bushel.)

CHAPTER 6

The Giveaway of Our Natural Resources

Logging and Our National Forests

In describing our Alaskan National Forest, *The Living Wilderness* (Jan.-Mar. 1976) states: "Tongass with its beautiful mountains, glaciers, and rainforest and its wealth of wildlife, is one of the nation's greatest natural assets."

Few can realize the extent of the stripping of this majestic area. Hundreds of thousands of acres of its timber are clear cut — not to build American homes, but for export to Japan. Much the same story may be told of forests in our northwestern states.

Allen Cowan, in *The Charlotte Observer* (6/1/82), quotes Denny Shaffer as saying he was appalled at what he saw in the national forest in Oregon in 1968 — a scarred landscape of tree stumps and eroding soil that resembled "a disaster."

In early October 1980, under pressure of lobbyists for lumber companies, a Congressional bill was passed allowing the cutting of timber in the North Carolina portion of the national forest.

In Asheville a government-paid operator with a computer is busy laying out plans for logging roads through the North Carolina natural forest. These roads are built at taxpayer expense. (The *Reader's Digest* for July 1983 states that an additional $50 million has been requested from Congress to build logging roads, and, further, that this is 11 percent of the money used for this purpose.) In North Carolina thousands of acres of priceless virgin timber are being clear cut. Where no reforestation planting follows, erosion will be disastrous.

For generations the people have bought, developed and cherished their natural forests — the wildlife, the rivers, the trails, the quiet, scenic beauty. There is peace there, a place where weary people can commune with nature and refresh their souls. Large areas of such forests should not be exploited for corporate profit.

Our Vast Wealth

On December 21, 1976, it was reported that the government estimates $2 trillion of oil lies beneath its outer continental shelf. And then there is the nation's gas, coal and uranium.

It is now known that the eight Rocky Mountain states: Montana, Wyoming, Idaho, Nevada, Utah, Colorado, Arizona, and New Mexico also have vast deposits of oil, shale (that contains more oil than all the Middle East), coal and uranium. (A splendid article on the natural resources of these states may be read in December 1980 edition of *Time.*)

The *Time* article states that of the 864,524 square miles, our government owns nearly half of the land and some 80 percent of the natural resources.

The same magazine article, "Life in Oil City, USA,"

states that around Evanston, Wyoming, oil flows out of the earth. Oil companies are taking it over. Said one official, "We will be here years — we haven't even found the end of this thing yet."

In these states, the government owns many thousand square miles of coal in seams of from eight to several hundred feet thick. This is a vast amount of wealth — wealth beyond dreams.

If these resources were kept and leased to operating companies for a fair share of the profits, they would greatly help with our taxes.

This vast wealth is being handed out for nothing to financiers who own the operating companies. (The small amounts of money they pay the government are recovered by raising the price of the product.) The corporations then use their monopoly on these necessities of life to exact the highest possible price from the people.

In the early 70's the supply of oil was plentiful; the prices, low. By October of 1973 the Organization of Petroleum Exporting Countries (OPEC) had 56% of world oil production, and supplied some 17.3% of American oil. In *A Time for Truth,* William E. Simon commented on the total amount of oil imports from all sources in this way: "We were by then importing 30 percent of our oil, and the national security implications were disturbing."

How disturbing we found out when the U.S. backed the Israelis in the Yom Kippur War of 1973. Immediately the Arabs slapped an embargo on oil against our nation.

On Dan Rather's "60 Minutes," followed by an article in *The Christian Science Monitor* (5/3/80), it was stated that former Undersecretary George W. Ball and former Treasury Secretary William E. Simon gave the following report on David Rockefeller's right-hand man. It seems that Henry Kissinger persuaded the Iranian

Shah to buy billions of dollars worth of arms, and raise the price of oil to pay for them. They did not tell Henry Kissinger's motive in this, nor did they tell whether Henry Kissinger encouraged the embargo.

It did not just involve the Shah. The embargo was widespread and well organized. If the oil-producing countries wanted to raise the price of oil, why didn't they just raise it, as they have many times since? They wanted to sell the oil. There was no reason why they should withhold it. The oil companies had a reason.

Are we to believe that the oil companies stumbled into the ensuing vast wealth by accident — or — did they plan it?

The threat to our nation all but eliminated competition from independent dealers. It forced the surrender of the nation's oil reserves. It forced permission for the Alaskan pipeline. It opened the way for the many leases of oil which have been granted since then — the nation's oil, which as we shall see, the oil companies get for nothing.

In that year of our need, the oil companies exported much more domestic oil than they had exported the year before. Later, when questioned about this, an oil company official answered that it was good business; that whereas their headquarters were in the United States, the corporations were multinational and owed no special homage to this country. Their "good business" shut us down almost completely.

The crisis brought results. A bill authorizing the Alaskan pipeline was signed November 16, 1973.

The Arab export ban was lifted March 18, 1974, with the price quintupled. At the time newspapers reported that our oil companies instigated the increase in price.

Following the embargo, our Federal Energy Administration, largely composed of men from the oil industry, divided currently pumped American oil into two classes. "Old oil" was defined as oil from any given well equal in volume to oil produced by the same well in the corresponding month of 1972. Its ceiling was raised from its low price to $5.25 a barrel.

It has been shown that some oil companies, falsifying records, claimed that "old oil" was "new," adding many billions of dollars to their wealth.

Later, in data prepared for grand jury investigation, it was charged that some major oil companies had, in some cases, set up as many as six or more dummy corporations for the purpose of selling oil at a profit, back and forth, to pad its price. In one instance, it was charged, this increase was from $5.50 a barrel, which the parent company had paid, to $25 a barrel charged utility companies, and passed on to the general public.

When the embargo was lifted in March of 1974, oil prices had risen from $2.10 to almost $10 a barrel: five times.

Oil prices crept up with inflation until a second energy crisis in 1979, caused by the Iranian revolution. They jumped from $13.34 in 1979 to nearly $34 per barrel in 1982. The bar graph below shows that rise, and the dramatic drop again by 1983.

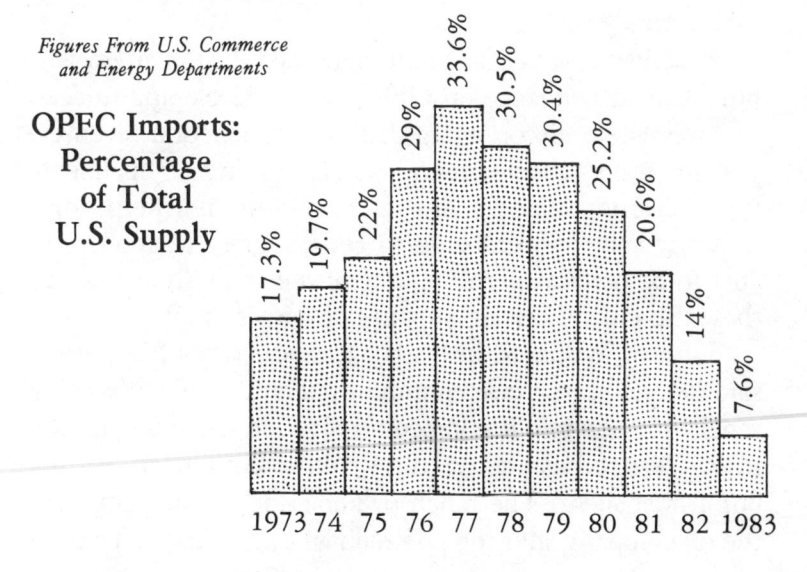

Figures From U.S. Commerce and Energy Departments

OPEC Imports: Percentage of Total U.S. Supply

1973	74	75	76	77	78	79	80	81	82	1983
17.3%	19.7%	22%	29%	33.6%	30.5%	30.4%	25.2%	20.6%	14%	7.6%

The western world learned some painful lessons through these experiences, and conservation became widespread. Today OPEC's share of world oil production is only 35%, the U.S. part of that only 7.6%! Now the gloom of the West has been transferred to OPEC. There is an oil glut worldwide, and oil-exporting nations have had to cut production back so far that most are experiencing government deficits now.

The *World Press Review* devoted several pages of its September 1983 issue to this phenomenon. Although "Saudi Arabia and Kuwait alone command more than $250 billion in foreign exchange reserves . . . the world no longer lives in fear of the Arabs," *The Times of India* is quoted as reporting.

Der Spiegel of Germany, quoted in the same issue of *WPR*, says of those two nations: "Kuwait, which had a budget surplus of $3.5 billion in 1981, had a $2.5-billion deficit in 1982 and forecasts a $4-billion deficit for 1984. Oil superpower Saudi Arabia has a deficit of more than $10 billion this year."

Meanwhile, our giant multinational oil companies, who built U.S. dependence on OPEC oil by developing mideast reserves while discouraging domestic production (even exporting some), had other plans. Designing a pipeline to bring oil from Alaska's vast reserves of her northern slope, they used the '73 embargo to get Congress to approve it. Just to be certain that no easing of the crisis should occur, they also cut off certain supplies of domestic oil.

Lindsey Williams, in his book, *The Energy Non-Crisis,* said he had seen a large pump in operation on a Wyoming ranch. He was told it pumped oil through the chief pipeline from West to East, across the Rockies. On a later visit the pump was silent. The ranch owner told Mr. Williams that the oil company shut the pump down during the oil crisis of the fall of 1973.

In those days cars formed long lines at filling stations. Owners drove them away with three gallons of gasoline, or none. While this was going on, tankers, loaded with oil, were anchored off our coasts, waiting for the inevitable advance in oil prices.

The graph below, based on figures released in 1983 by the U.S. Departments of Commerce and Energy, tells a dramatic story. At the time of the Arab embargo in 1973, U.S. dependence upon OPEC oil was 17.3%. As of the first quarter of 1983, it had fallen to 7.6%, after rising to a high of 33.6% in 1977. Clearly, conservation measures such as insulating buildings and driving compact cars have had their effect.

Per Barrel Price of OPEC Crude Oil

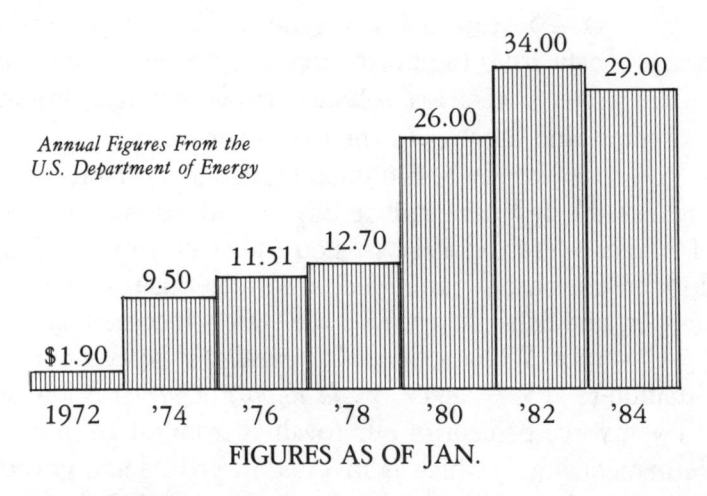

Annual Figures From the U.S. Department of Energy

Year	Price
1972	$1.90
'74	9.50
'76	11.51
'78	12.70
'80	26.00
'82	34.00
'84	29.00

FIGURES AS OF JAN.

In some countries government-owned natural resources are used for the good of all their people.

In Alberta, the oil-rich province of Canada, the government receives a handsome royalty from drillers of this oil, and uses this money for government expenses.

Taxes are low. Per capita income is among the highest on earth. Everywhere there is an air of prosperity. Alberta is not piling up debt for future generations — quite the opposite. She is putting a third of her oil income into a trust for the future — for citizens yet unborn.

There is no income tax in Kuwait. Its great wealth is for its people.

The *U.S. News & World Report* states that Oman's oil wealth "... has brought the state a stream of schools, hospitals, housing, highways and modern communications."

How different from the way our natural resources are handled here, in the United States of America! Could they not be handled in *all* our states as they are now in Alaska?

Alaska

Alaska, 25 years old as a state in 1984, has received much benefit from the north slope oil: $6 billion spent on public projects such as schools, roads, sewage systems, museums, and libraries in the past seven years.

Ex-governor Jay S. Hammond stated in a personal letter that, for the original Prudhoe Bay oil and gas sale, the state of Alaska "received $900 million and one-eighth royalty." Former Governor Hammond, a former bush pilot, poet, trapper, and fisherman, ended the state's income tax.

Governor William Sheffield revealed Alaska's current situation to *U.S. News & World Report* (1/9/84) as follows: "Twenty-five percent of our royalties from oil go into the Permanent Fund, which is invested in private and government securities. The fund is now close to $5 billion and earned about $404 million in 1983. Half of that dividend is paid out to the people of Alaska — $386.15 per person last year. The rest goes back into the fund, which we expect to reach nearly $10 billion by 1990."

The governor went on to say that the Permanent Fund would be needed when the Prudhoe Bay earnings start dropping in 1990.

In preparation for that day, the huge oil companies are making some desperate moves. Recently Texaco invested $1.7 billion into leases and exploratory drilling in the Mukluk area of the Bering Sea. According to *U.S. News and World Report* (1/23/84), "The well yielded mostly water."

Perhaps in reaction to such a loss, Texaco recently bought Getty Oil for $9.9 billion. *U.S. News and World Report* says, "By acquiring Getty, Texaco will be able to double its oil reserves for about $6 a barrel, compared with an average cost of $14 a barrel to go out and find it. . . . Some analysts see oil mergers as a huge gamble . . . the merger saddles Texaco with huge borrowing costs, which could be ruinous if oil prices slump. Loan interest alone could equal all of Texaco's earnings" *(ibid.).*

In addition to gobbling up smaller companies and making competition nearly impossible for independent oil companies, the giant oil companies have been spending on other investments — not research and development.

In Florida there are, from time to time, reports of oil company purchases of Florida investment property. On April 10, 1977, there came a report that Gulf Oil Real Estate Company would build an additional cluster of 80 apartments at their 120-acre ocean-front development area on Hutchinson Island, Fort Pierce.

This will be their fifth section of apartments at that location. Such outside investments must be going on all over the nation.

Only two days before, Paul Harvey had stated that the holding company which owns Sinclair Oil had purchased one of the nation's largest ski slopes. In 1977, also, Atlantic Richfield bought Anaconda Copper Company. In the years since then there have been many such reports.

It is reported that Gulf Oil attempted to buy Ringling Brothers Circus. It bid on a giant Chicago financial company; it has invested in real estate and has built the town of Reston, Virginia; it has bought chemical companies; and has opened a chain of auto parts and service stores. Mobil Oil paid hundreds of millions of dollars for the controlling interest in Marcor, parent company of Montgomery-Ward.

Deregulation

The oil and natural gas beneath government land should be a resource for all our people. Until recently, oil leases on such lands benefited taxpayers.

Foreign oil imports did not become a factor until multinational corporations forced U.S. dependency on their overseas investments, early in the 70's. Now the pendulum is swinging back from reliance upon imports. In 1973 the U.S. imported six million barrels of oil a day; in 1983 imports were only 4.3 million barrels a day *(U.S. News and World Report,* 10/24/83).

Until 1979, the price an oil company could charge for its finished product was regulated by government.

All through that year, President Carter lambasted the oil companies for their unconscionable greed. Yet, despite the fact that the April 24, 1979, report of oil companies' profits showed increases of from 65 to more than 200 percent above the same period of the year before, he, on June 1, 1979, deregulated the price of 80 percent of oil. Newscasts showed the signing. President Carter looked up, sideways, and said of the "windfall profit tax": "The oil companies will have to pay this tax — the people will not have to pay it," as if all additional costs of any product are not passed on to consumers.

This deregulation allowed oil companies to set their own price on imported oil, and on all domestic oil but that from the old wells. Therefore, consumers ended up paying exorbitant prices even on oil extracted from government-leased lands! Over the next ten years the people will pay the oil companies an additional trillion dollars' profit. A "windfall profits tax" will be levied on this — a little over a fourth — $277 billion. The people *will* pay this — first to the oil companies. Some of this tax will go to the poor, to make the deal palatable. Much of the balance will be returned to the oil companies in tax breaks and cash.

After deregulation of the price of oil there was an enormous increase in inflation with its high interest rates. It is worthy of note that the Rockefellers are interested in oil and in banking, and that through government action these businesses are reaping enormous profits while the rest of the nation's economy, paying these high prices, is in shambles.

Exxon Oil Company profits continued their dazzling climb in 1980: its profits for the first quarter were 101.6 percent higher than for the same quarter the year before. Chase Manhattan Bank profits for 1979 were 58 percent higher than they were for 1978.

Is it any wonder that in one case published in the *Asheville Citizen* (12/23/79) a legacy of $20 million in oil company stock became a legacy of from $40 to $50 million in the two years it took to settle the estate?

While the Iron Is Hot

And now the government has leased Georges Bank to the oil companies — 660,000 acres of the richest fishing area in the world. The taxpayers' potentially rich oil deposits there will be sold for a comparative trifle which the people will pay in the end.

On July 21, 1982, the federal government announced that it would lease the entire Atlantic and Pacific coastal waters to oil and gas companies. About one billion acres will be leased in 41 lease sales through June, 1987.

The *U.S. News & World Report* (6/6/83) stated that the Department of Interior had leased, for drilling, 5,000 square miles of prime oil and gas waters, shallow and calm, in the Gulf of Mexico, for $3.5 billion.

With their enormous profits, while the nation still reels from the "oil crisis," the financiers are hurrying to buy up all possible sources of energy. They are not setting their sights on the oil they can pump in the next decade, and the next; they want title to it all — NOW!

The Proposal to Reduce Our Maritime Fleet

When the size of the Alaskan pipeline was first announced, many people were disturbed. The pipe was to be much larger than needed to supply the West Coast. There were rumors that the plan was to ship oil to Japan. The oil companies assured us that they would ship all surplus oil through the Panama Canal to our East Coast.

On September 21, 1976, company officials reported that their experts, usually so infallible, had made a serious mistake — that the surplus would be from 100,000 to 600,000 barrels of oil a day — too much for the Canal. They could think of no solution save to ship this excess oil to Japan. These officials said that our oil would be exchanged for oil that the Japanese would buy from the Arabs, to be delivered to our East Coast. Therefore the companies requested the Senate's permission to ship this oil to Japan.

Had this been the secret plan all along? It is calculated by analysts that this exchange may result in $182 million a year additional profit. Who would get the money? Once hauling started, who could be trusted to monitor the exchange? Is this to be another case in which large amounts of the nation's vital oil will be exported for greater profit — as it was in 1973?

According to *The Spotlight* (11/9/81), this subject surfaced again. This time it was a campaign to persuade the Reagan Administration and Congress to transfer the shipping of the Alaskan oil from American-owned tankers to tankers owned and operated by the Japanese and other foreigners.

By the summer of 1983, Japan was threatening to sell more cars here unless we sent this oil to them, according to *Spotlight* (8/1/83). Failing here, they evaded the Foreign Agent Registration Act by hiring an American-born Japanese, furnishing money to lobby our government to sell them this oil. The newspaper said that President Reagan was in favor of this sale.

It is claimed that cheaper foreign labor would save money for the oil companies. It would scrap or mothball 50 American tankers, and idle 3,600 American seamen. Russia has the largest maritime fleet in the world. Japan is next and is rapidly building. The United States is tenth.

In December of 1983, Thomas J. O'Hara, editor of *The Professional Mariner,* made an impassioned plea for two bills presently before the Congress. He stated that the Reagan administration is opposed to them, as follows.

"Number one on the Administration's hit list is H.R. 1241, sponsored by Rep. Lindy Boggs (D-LA), and its companion, S. 1624, sponsored by Sen. Paul Trible (R-VA) — both of which would eventually reserve 20 percent of U.S. bulk cargoes for U.S.-built, U.S.-crewed vessels. All the while, however, President Reagan's men continue to affirm their support for cargo preference laws already on the books. . . .

"The American merchant marine carried 80 percent of

our men and supplies overseas in World War II. The percentage was 95 percent during Korea and Vietnam. . . . The Navy estimates that, given the current sealift capacities of the U.S. fleet, if their proposed 600-ship fleet requisitioned the *entire* merchant fleet under U.S. flag, there would still be a shortage of nearly 350 ships necessary to sustain it. . . .

"The maritime industry . . . is puzzled and angry over the Administration's arbitrary policy. The farm bloc sniffs that the merchant marine should, in the words of George Berg of the American Farm Bureau Federation, 'pull themselves up by their own bootstraps.' Perhaps the agriculture industry with its $24.5 billion in subsidies (up 569% since 1980) will show the maritime industry ($360 *million, down* 34%) how, George? Both industries are suffering from the effects of unfair subsidized competition and high interest rates. The country could procure the same products and services provided by the two from overseas for less money. But the survival of both is necessary for the well-being of the U.S.''

Perhaps the reader will have more than raised eyebrows that our congressmen have to fight for a bill to *"eventually* reserve 20 percent of U.S. bulk cargoes for U.S. vessels.'' A phone call to Mr. O'Hara, the author of the preceding article, revealed that, at present, *less than two percent of American bulk cargoes are transported by U.S. crews and vessels!*

A friend who has stood on a levy in New Orleans and watched ships with the hammer and sickle on them sailing up our Mississippi River knows what this means. She describes her feeling of helplessness in this way, as her host explained that Soviet ships were sailing up north to get our grain.

"Although I had read about U.S. sales of grain to the USSR, it never came home to me until that moment. Knowing that the ship before me was doubtless filled with sophisticated spying technology, sold by multinationals to our enemies who have vowed to bury us, I realized America is being destroyed by its Fifth Column within. Also knowing that much of our grain goes to produce liquor for the huge number of Soviet alcoholics, I cried out to God to change this mess — for it is obvious that our government since Yalta will not.''

Natural Gas

Natural gas supplies about one-third of the nation's energy.

Those who own the great oil companies own most of the gas companies and market much of the nation's natural gas. There have been long, determined efforts to throw off price control.

In 1974 the Federal Power Commission set a nationwide pipeline price of forty-two cents per thousand cubic feet. This was raised to 50 cents and was to be advanced one cent a year.

The producers demanded more. Relying on estimates furnished by producers, the Commission advanced the price.

In November 1976 the price stood at $1.01 for gas from old wells and $1.42 for gas from wells drilled after 1974. It was estimated that the advance cost the consumer some $1.5 to $1.75 billion a year.

In the dreadful winter of 1977, gas was in short supply. Schools were closed. Factories were shut down, throwing tens, perhaps hundreds of thousands of people out of work. There were many reports of suffering and death. The price of gas to users was staggering. A story, which must have had many counterparts, was told of the financial straits of one family — a father, mother and four children. The following figures are roughly correct. The family income was a little over $400 a month. Payments on their home were $100, and their gas bill was $200.

Most of the natural gas in the Gulf is produced in areas leased by the federal government. There came rumors that gas companies were withholding this gas, and in some cases switching gas in the pipes to those who paid the higher prices.

In the middle of February, 1977, a government probe charged that a large amount of the Gulf of Mexico natural gas was easily available but secretly held back. The gas companies contended that they could not afford to drill for this supply at the price of gas then. Give them a higher rate, they said, and there would be plenty of gas. The gas companies also said that a large increase in rates was not excessive, for they feared that the time would come when, because of lessening supply, their profits would be lower.

All through that time the gas companies were publishing reports that the nation would deplete its supply of natural gas in twenty or thirty years.

In 1977 President Carter asked Congress to phase out price control on natural gas and allow the price to rise until they were, in energy, the equal of the price of oil. A complicated compromise bill came from Congress in November 1978.

This bill allowed prices of gas from old wells — those drilled before April 20, 1977 — to reach the well-head price of $1.90 per thousand cubic feet by 1985. The price of gas from wells drilled since then may reach $4.54 per thousand cubic feet at that time, and gas from wells drilled after that time shall be priced at the world market price of gas.

Then came other estimates of the amount of natural gas the United States government owns.

In 1979 enormous quantities of natural gas were

reported discovered in the Gulf coast of Texas and Louisiana. "The U.S. sits atop a gas bonanza." Since then it has transpired that there are enormous deposits of natural gas along the Alaskan coast, in the eight Rocky Mountain states, and along the Appalachian range — mostly on government land. Some of the gas is deep, but there is enough to last far into the future.

The gas companies are doing well. They are extending their pipeline every day. Since 1977 the price of gas has advanced 27 percent each year.

Despite this, President Reagan wants to deregulate the price of gas, as he did of oil, and allow the gas companies to set their own price — in energy equivalent to the price of oil.

The present price of gas is about one-third the price of oil. Gas is used by some 43,000,000 families in the United States. When decontrol is complete, either now or in 1985, the added cost to each of these families may reach near $2,000 each year — some $86 billion additional profit to the gas companies.

In December 1981, President Reagan signed a law which permitted gas companies to begin now to charge customers to raise $43 billion to build an Alaskan pipeline for gas. Most of the $110 billion profit will go to the promoters — not to the people who own the gas.

On the CBS newscast, September 9, 1982, it was stated that there is an excessive amount of gas — so much that large companies had stopped buying from small ones, and these were burning gas in the fields. Despite this, the gas companies have raised prices — as much as 30 to 70 percent in some cities.

Coal

The power companies (in the time of President Eisenhower and President Nixon) failed in their efforts to take over the government's enormous and vital gaseous diffusion plants at Oak Ridge. They then bought the mines which supply coal to these plants, and greatly increased the price of this fuel.

Despite the fact that our government (that is, all of our citizens) owned, in the west, an enormous amount of sulphur-free coal, Oak Ridge continued to pay these high prices.

Not only this but, clouded in secrecy, our officials leased vast areas of these western coal deposits to corporations owned by the bankers, Exxon, and other oil companies, for as little as $1 an acre and royalties of from 17-1/2¢ to 25¢ a ton.

On August 10, 1976, Congress overrode President Ford's veto and raised the price for leasing coal on federal land to 12½ percent of its value. The President said the advance in price was harmful — that it would probably be passed on to consumers.

The incident brings to mind the plain fact that every lease or sale of our natural resources to such companies, our oil, coal, uranium, timber, is a gift. The companies simply raise the price of the finished product, and thus force consumers to pay for all costs.

In certain states, especially Montana, the price of coal has been advanced to these companies, but even here the above statement still stands.

Montana has learned its lesson. It has been stripped of its natural resources before. (In 1980 Anaconda Copper Company began to send its copper to Japan to be smelted and began phasing out its plant, leaving Butte, once the richest hill on earth, with a "gasping pit," *The Christian Science Monitor,* 8/12/81).

The *New York Times* of May 1, 1983, stated that with a glut of federal coal — leases sufficient to furnish coal for the next 20 to 25 years — the Department of the Interior was making new leases of vast tracts of government coal land. Says Geoffrey Webb, of the Earth Environment Group: "massive amounts of public wealth are being transferred to private hands, very quickly and very cheaply."

"It furnishes jobs," we are told. Yes it does, subsistence for the laborers — as long, and only as long as they dig out federal treasure and hand it to enormously wealthy financiers.

From 3,000 to 5,000 people apply for 80 jobs; 1,000 stood in line all night (UPI photo).

Jobs

Jobs! For most of us it is always jobs. The President, the financiers, the great corporations hold jobs before us — the carrot. The stick of privation, of hunger and despair is in the background. Such jobs are devised and given by the wealthy to create more wealth for the wealthy. There is nothing benevolent about jobs. Even as the laborers toil, the wealthy seek more automation, and carry their jobs overseas.

Jobs, in practice, are not as easy to get, to work at and to hold as one might think — judging by the lightness and ease with which the word is spoken. Read the inscription under the picture on the facing page. Long lines of people seeking work are not uncommon.

On a CBS newcast the night of July 18, 1981, there was shown a scene of darkness. Then the shifting, selective beam of a photographer's spotlight illuminated a portion of such a line. Each man in the line stood motionless, waiting for the morrow, hoping that he would be one of those chosen for the few available jobs.

A latecomer arrived and attempted to force his way into the line. We watched the struggle and fight as the photographer tried to keep the eerie scene in view.

We all know the meaning of "a job": its sometime weariness; the monotony of a routine task repeated day after day after day; year after year. We know, at firsthand what Iago meant when he spoke of one who:

"Wears out his time, much like his master's ass,
For naught but provender."

There is no life so fearful as that which is at the total mercy of some coercive master.

Is it heresy to want some of the wealth?

CHAPTER 7

Utilities

For utilities a regional monopoly is guaranteed by law.
Profit is also guaranteed by law. This profit is based on a percentage of the utilities' appraised value. As inflation raises the monetary estimate of the value of a utility company, the Utility Commission or the courts often adjust the percentage rate upward.

Power and Light Companies

Power and light companies almost constantly demand and receive advances in rates.

They tell us that fuel has increased in cost several times in the past few years, and that interest is high. They do not tell us that their controlling stock is owned by great northern banks in the names of nominees, insurance companies and the like, and owned by the men who own the oil companies, the natural gas, and the coal mines. Nor do they tell us that those great banks could furnish the bank credit for expansion, and set their own interest rate.

As if they were the government itself, the power and

light companies exercise the right of eminent domain to condemn (declare converted to public use) and take the choicest, most prized valleys, not only for their lakes but for their large power lines. They then send highly trained agents, in pairs, to offer a pittance for such property. These agents return time and again, argue by the hour, yell and storm, beat the coffee table with their fists, threaten and browbeat the owner to secure his property for the lowest possible dollar. (This I learned by personal experience.)

This was not because they couldn't have taken another route on my same farm, shorter, and offered for nothing. Their agents said they wanted it through a cultivated field so the company would not have the expense of keeping down undergrowth. The power companies lay claim to the God-given rain and the flowing streams.

Depression or no depression, a power company's profits, supposedly based on a percentage of the value of its physical plants, are guaranteed by law. In times of inflation these plants, no matter what they had cost, are appraised higher and higher, and the rate for electricity is correspondingly increased.

Other factors come into the charges for electricity.

Since the oil crises we have been constantly urged to use less electricity. We do: by insulating, putting in storm windows, turning off lights and using appliances less. This does not lower our electric bill. The rate is increased to give the company the same income. Should the overall use of electricity be reduced by one-half, a customer who then used as much as before must pay twice as much for it.

Taxes that an electric company are supposed to pay are added in and paid by the users. The companies do not pay all of this to the government.

In their company publications of October 1975, both Duke Power Company and Carolina Power and Light Company answered the charge that with combined reported profits of $172.2 million, they had paid no federal tax for 1974. The answer, they said, lay in their system of bookkeeping. No tax was due. Although they made the profit in money, it was considered, after allowance for funds used during construction, and after accelerated depreciation, to be not profit but a part of a large loss. In the case of the Carolina Power and Light Company, the $72.2 million earned became a $44 million loss — for use against next year's taxes.

And further, the stockholders (chiefly northern banks) who had been paid large dividends, didn't have to pay federal tax on them either. It was, the company officials said, as if the stockholders' own money had been returned to them.

Also added in is money for new plants — paid for by the people who furnish the money.

Proof of this statement is often confirmed by the utility companies. A typical example was heard on an ABC newscast, August 26, 1981. It was stated that Duke Power Company was asking for a 20-percent rate hike. A spokesman for the company said that unless this increase were granted, the company could not meet the needs of future consumers; that the money was needed to build another atomic power plant.

In February, 1982, the Carolina Power and Light Company asked for an increase of 13 percent. Part of the money, officials of the company said, would be used to build a new plant.

There is a deeper meaning to all this. Following the small investments creating the early utility companies, these utilities have had a steady accumulation of assets. Their customers, the people who have used the utilities, have not only paid for service; they have paid for most of the expansion which have produced the giant utilities of our day — capital now used in the calculation of rates.

Utility companies are closely related, privately, with state officials on utility commissions. There are incidences where these companies employ, as attorneys, members of the state Legislature who regulate them. Commissioners who grant increases in rates are often employed by these companies when their terms of office with the government is over.

The price of electricity continues to rise. On WLOS TV, Asheville, N.C., December 15, 1981, it was announced that Carolina Power and Light Company had been granted another increase of 13 percent. This increased the average monthly electrical bill by $7. On December 17, 1981, Duke Power and Light Company was granted an increase of 15 percent. Both asked for and received raises in 1982. This has been repeated time and again.

Early in March, 1982, it was reported that in parts of California the electric bill had doubled and tripled in the previous three months.

Yet all of this happened at a time when the cost of oil was decreasing. In the recent recession the rest of the population accepted lower wages and tightened their belts, but not the utilities.

James Schlesinger, former government energy chief, put into words what everybody knows: that those who own energy are insatiable; that no matter how many times their prices are advanced, that no matter what concessions are made to them, there will always be a demand for more.

Telephones

We have a wonderful telephone system. Anyone can lift a receiver, begin to punch in his number, and almost by the time the last numeral is pressed, hear the ring of a telephone three thousand miles away. We paid well for this good service and were pleased to do so. And now, it is said, that the government, to break up a monopoly, has divided the American Telephone and Telegraph Company into several parts.

The chief owners of the stock in the undivided system are the chief owners of stock in the new order. The company goes to great lengths in advertisement, to tell why we should now pay an enormous increase for the service — as if this is forced upon the company.

The several regional Bell systems say that as part of the whole they were subsidized by excess profits from AT&T long-distance calls, and that now, split off from this, they will not get this help. In order to operate, they will need higher rates and more money.

The parent, American Telephone and Telegraph Company, says that now, since long-distance calls are all it has, it needs monthly entrance fees from those who wish to use long-distance phones, and also higher rent on telephones.

If a government, to protect the public from overcharge by some giant monopolistic corporation, dismembers it, one would think that prices of its goods or services would be lowered, not raised. Is this enormous advance in price another accident, or did highly paid company executives think it all up, and lobbyists and attorneys put it over? Is this a sample of what to expect when our government breaks up other monopolies?

All of this is rather confusing. The following is clear enough. On ABC's newscast, December 21, 1983, it was reported that AT&T has bought a billion-dollar company in Europe and is going international.

AT&T's great ads are seen in many magazines. A two-page one in *U.S. News & World Report* for January 16, 1984, states: "Now we're free from many restrictions that bound us in the past. We're free to compete and eager to. Not just in America, but around the world."

CHAPTER 8

The Pentagon

One would think that here, at the Pentagon, entrusted with the protection of the nation, one would find efficiency, patriotism, high honor and selflessness, among both those in charge and the contractors they deal with. But no.

In the spring of 1969 partial disclosures showed that 61 House members, including some of the Armed Services and Appropriations Committee, were stockholders in corporations having major defense contracts. There were no disclosures for the Senate. Many congressmen have Reserve commissions in the military. A panel to investigate the Defense Department consisted of 15 members. Eight of these represented businesses that had defense contracts of more than $100 million apiece. Two more were interested in the stock of these companies.

Officials of high rank in the Pentagon who hand out the contracts are nearing retirement. If their relationships are good, there is a chance for later employment in the armament factories. *The Charlotte Observer* quotes Senator Proxmire as reporting that the nation's top 100 defense contractors with $26 billion in Pentagon contracts have

2,072 retired military officers on their payrolls.

Since World War II Congress has appropriated about two trillion dollars for defense. A large part of this has been wasted. In A. Ernest Fitzgerald's *The High Priests of Waste,* the author said the Pentagon discharged him when he testified to this waste before a Congressional committee. Conditions have not changed. On May 14, 1981, Jack Anderson stated that in 1980 almost 65 percent of the money the Pentagon spent for armament went to contractors who were the only bidders. Billions of dollars are wasted on overcharges, stretched out contract time, and shoddy workmanship.

Our financiers are abandoning many home markets as being beneath their notice. They are also losing many markets because of shoddy merchandise and built-in obsolescence. They have specialized in the more lucrative manufacture of arms and other munitions of war. Payments for these are guaranteed by the sale of interest-bearing United States bonds. The price here is not questioned; the more the better. An electric switch knob worth a few cents or dollars is called an electronic control device and priced at over a hundred dollars. A ten-cent article, in stock, is bought at a cost of over a hundred dollars; a $14.73 hammer is bought at over $400. In just four years the projected cost of a B-1 bomber has increased from $25 million to $75 million. Officials of corporations with defense companies contribute large amounts to the President and to congressmen.

General Dynamics, with a two-billion-dollar contract, charged $325,000 for a report that was not delivered. One cruise missile contractor charged $1 million for a special data list which should have cost $40,000. When confronted with this, the contractor blamed it on a typographical error.

Congress and the Pentagon have had plenty of time to

correct this evil, but it is still with us. The *Asheville Citizen* (9/4/83) quotes Steward L. Storms, a technician at the Lomore Naval Air Station in California, as testifying before Congress that Sperry sold diodes to the Navy that could have been bought for 4 cents, for $110. And again, the bill to replace a $237 air filter was $1730. The *U.S. News & World Report* (11/14/83) reports that the Pentagon paid $9,600 for a 12-cent wrench; $18,000 for a sofa.

Whole sections of our country have grown dependent on armament factory payrolls. Defense contractors employ millions of workers.

Hundreds of lobbyists and public relations experts are employed and millions of dollars are spent to persuade us that this is right. Armament salesmen travel the world, carrying samples of weapons and moving picture films of simulated warfare, brochures and the like, and make elaborate presentations to sell their wares. Much of this armament is given as foreign aid and charged to the American taxpayer.

Secretary Schlesinger stated February 27, 1974, that the then enormous Pentagon budget, near $90 billion, was designed, "in part" to stimulate a faltering economy. Some economists say that to stop waste too many men would be thrown out of work. The answer for now is that thousands of articles now made abroad and imported should be made at home.

"No one has ever succeeded in keeping nations at war except by lies."

Salvador de Madariaga

CHAPTER 9

The Arch-Criminals

It has been truly said that the greatest crimes are not committed by violent men with blackjacks, knives and pistols in darkened streets. They are committed by quiet, well-mannered, highly educated men, sitting around conference tables in beautifully paneled and appointed board rooms.

It is there that crafty, secret plans are made to wheedle billions of dollars in "overruns" from the people. And it is there — for a profit — that the vote for war is cast, sending millions to their deaths.

It has not been through coincidence that our peaceful people have, time after time, been betrayed by their leaders — elected upon promise to keep them out of war — secretly plotting all the while with financiers to plunge the nation into war, under the pretext of enforcing peace.

In *An Editor's Notebook,* John A. Knight said:

"Historically, and I speak only of this century, official deception has been a standard tool of international diplomacy and intrigue. It has brought on wars at frightful cost of blood and resources."

He goes on to tell how President Wilson, elected upon a

peace platform, maneuvered the United States into World War I; how Franklin Roosevelt was elected upon a peace platform and then, without the knowledge of the American people, maneuvered us into World War II; how John Kennedy went into Vietnam, stating that a treaty called for it; how Lyndon Johnson enlarged that war, and how Richard Nixon used S.E.A.T.O. as his excuse to continue it.

Of course, these Presidents, of themselves, would not have led this country into these terrible conflicts. Surrounding circumstances tell us that there was a tacit understanding, if not an actual pledge to financiers, in return for the money that put them into office.

There are profits in wars; profits in the manufacture of munitions and other equipments of war; and there is profit in the natural resources and markets of the nations we are "protecting."

These profits go to those who already have more than they could use in a thousand lifetimes: those whose sons do not go into battle.

The following refers to World War II:

> "During the five-year period from 1939 to 1944, bank deposits more than doubled in amount, an increase that was entirely due to purchase of government securities by the banks. From less than one-fifth in 1939, government securities had become more than two-thirds of the earning assets of the banks."
> *Encyclopaedia Britannica,* 1949 Edition

America's total bill for World War II was 294,000 dead and some $318 billion. (It should not be forgotten that this war cost all sides 17 million military and 18 million civilian lives.)

The Vietnam War cost this nation 58,000 dead, 340,000

The flower of our nation lie in fields such as this (Omaha Beach, France, UPI photo).

wounded and some $140 billion in money. No one can estimate what the final bill will be. The whole country was torn apart. Its moral fabric was weakened, its dollar devalued. By and large the war was conducted in secrecy and deception.

Our people struggle with a wrecked economy and pay interest on government bonds that were issued. They also have to listen to the statements of professional economists, that the inflation we now face could have been avoided if there had been a tax levied to pay for the war as it was being fought. Just who do these economists think should have paid the tax? The financiers, who were making enormous profits, and who avoid taxes? Or do the economists mean the working class whose backs were already breaking under their tax load?

To all this must be added the war's effect on our young men, on those who came back, the emotional trauma, the physical disability, the painful Agent-Orange poisoning, the returnee's economic despair. In April 1982 *The Christian Inquirer* stated that there have been 50,000 suicides among the Vietnam War veterans.

Present World Tension

Maps of the Near East and Africa show many little nations: their people poor, their earth rich with oil or minerals. Our internationalists were not content to let the people of these nations have their own natural resources. They were not willing to help, to guide, to bargain and deal fairly for these products. A mere handful of internationalists saw and wanted this wealth for themselves. By stirring up strife and selling arms, by bribery of officials, by the promise of jobs, they have taken a large share of these resources. Our nation, controlled and led by these internationalists, gradually came to depend on this oil and the minerals. They are vital.

The Soviet Union, seeing all this decided that they would, by fair means or foul, take these resources for themselves. They infiltrated countries and by giving arms and preaching their philosophy, implanted themselves. In the attempt to force us out they have built great offensive armaments. They arm guerrilla bands to overthrow governments.

As reported in the *Asheville Citizen-Times* (8/8/81), the Egyptian President Anwar Sadat, speaking before the Council on Foreign Relations, said that the United States and the Soviet Union should stop intervening in the domestic affairs of other nations.

He stated that such intervention is "A dangerous malaise that threatens the fabric of contemporary life."

A most significant utterance at the Cancun, Mexican summit was the appraisal of the American freedom by a Third World delegate quoted by *The Christian Science Monitor* (10/26/81): "And to us, their kind of freedom looks like the freedom of the lion to swallow the gazelle, the freedom of the multinationals to roam the world at will."

In this confrontation both super powers are putting forth all efforts to increase the armaments each has supplied to their dependents and allies. The world has become an armed camp. The double claim on these natural resources seems unresolvable.

CHAPTER 10

The Nation's Monetary System

It has been over seven decades since the financiers tricked the people into allowing them to inaugurate the Federal Reserve System: to create money by entering a line in a ledger and, along with it, exact government bonds dollar for dollar for the use of this money. The bonds did not stay in the Federal Reserve vaults; they drifted out, mostly into the hands of those who controlled the system.

Considering high interest and taxes, one might think that most of the bonds would have been canceled. But no. The financiers know how to avoid taxes. When the Federal Reserve began, the federal debt was a little over one billion dollars. It is now stated to be a trillion, four hundred billion dollars. There has never been an audit of the Federal Reserve. The nation's total indebtedness is over $12 trillion, according to the 1983 table published by the National Taxpayers Union which follows.

A handful of financiers who control this system have come to own most of the productive wealth of the nation openly; in fact, they have bonds and mortgages for most of the rest.

Taxpayer's Liability Index
prepared by
National Taxpayers Union
325 Pennsylvania Avenue, S.E.
Washington, D.C. 20003

YOUR ATTENTION IS DIRECTED TO AMOUNTS DUE AS INDICATED BELOW

DEBT OR LIABILITY ITEM	GROSS COST	YOUR SHARE*
Public Debt	$ 1,290,000,000,000	$ 16,125
Accounts Payable	$ 185,000,000,000	$ 2,312
Undelivered Orders	$ 516,000,000,000	$ 6,450
Long Term Contracts	$ 15,000,000,000	$ 187
Loan and Credit Guarantees	$ 346,000,000,000	$ 4,325
Insurance Commitments	$ 2,079,000,000,000	$ 25,988
Annuity Programs	$ 7,645,000,000,000	$ 95,563
Unadjudicated Claims International Commitments & other Financial Obligations	$ 81,000,000,000	$ 1,013
TOTAL	$12,157,000,000,000	$151,963

*Based on 80 million real taxpayers.

Deficit-Spending and Foreign Aid

A large national debt, evinced by interest-bearing United States bonds, is inherent in the Federal Reserve System. Much of the interest must be carried somewhere as a debt.

Deficit-spending provides payment for the financiers' products; for much that is sold to our government; those things given to other countries; for many things foreigners buy from our multinationals. Deficit-spending and foreign aid are constantly urged, and Congress authorizes it. Senator Jesse Helms (R-NC) says that since World War II the United States has sent over one trillion dollars in aid and credit to foreign countries.

Much of this foreign aid has gone into dictators' private bank accounts. A typical example of this is seen in the use of the money which for some 44 years we sent to Haile Salassie, Emperor of Ethiopia. It sustained him in splendor and furnished the power to keep his pitiful, half-starved people in subjugation.

Ryszard Kapuscihski, in "The Emperor" *(Time, 7/18/83)*, tells that during one of the Emperor's great feasts, there were, in the black night, at the garbage dump, a crowd of barefooted beggars ravenously eating fish heads, bones and scraps of food thrown out by the dishwashers.

Following the coup d'etat and execution of 60 corrupt, wealthy officials, the late Emperor Haile Salassie, himself a prisoner, thought it a good idea to yield his part of the booty. There were stocks and bonds, and gold bullion, jewels and money, most of which he had stashed in Swiss banks. The value ran into billions of dollars.

For all our aid, Ethiopia is now communistic and in Russia's camp.

Our Foreign Image

News today is flashed around the world. Do those in other countries who see and read it know of the stranglehold financiers have on our government? Do they know of the American taxpayers' debt? Do they realize that our prosperity is more apparent than real? Do they have reservations about our brand of capitalism?

Perhaps some in other countries have a more personal reason to hate us. Our internationalists, controlling our government, use taxpayer funds to make large gifts to corrupt rulers and supply them with arms. These are made in the financiers' factories and paid for by our people — all to curry favor and for permission to operate within their countries. Anti-American demonstrators, enraged at U.S. support for their corrupt and despotic rulers, often protest the multinational takeover of their natural resources — a pump that sucks out much of their wealth.

Instead of putting our own house in order and showing these countries what a true republic can be, instead of helping them gain their own freedom, we are letting our own slip away. We often watch helpless while the bankers and multinationals aid their despotic rulers. Then, when other nations cannot pay their loans to those bankers, such debts are placed on the backs of American taxpayers. Our tax system is the subject of the next chapter.

CHAPTER 11

Taxes

Early in 1984 President Reagan unveiled his budget for fiscal 1985: the largest in American history. The $925.5-billion budget projects a flood of red ink. Its $180.4-billion deficit is only slightly smaller than the giant deficits of the past two years.

How will most of this money be raised? By taxes. Here are figures on income and payment programs for fiscal 1983, 1984, and 1985. They were given to us by phone on February 23, 1984, by the Fiscal Analysis Division of the Office of Management and Budget in Washington.

Federal Income in Billions

YEARS:	1983	1984	1985
Personal Income Taxes	$289.9	$293.3	$328.4
Social Security Taxes	$183.0	$208.5	$236.7
Corporate Taxes	$ 37.0	$ 66.6	$ 76.5
All Other Taxes	$ 60.2	$ 67.4	$ 69.2
Other Revenue	$ 31.5	$ 34.3	$ 34.3
TOTAL	$600.6	$670.1	$745.1

Federal Payments in Billions

	1983	1984	1985
SOCIAL PROGRAMS: TOTAL	$412.0	$422.8	$440.6
Breakdown:			
Social Insurance & Retirement	$276.8	$283.0	$303.8
Welfare	$ 63.2	$ 63.6	$ 65.5
Aid to Veterans	$ 24.2	$ 25.1	$ 26.0
Community Development & Economic Aid	$ 19.5	$ 20.8	$ 16.3
Human Development & Services	$ 28.3	$ 30.3	$ 29.0
DEPARTMENT OF DEFENSE	$204.4	$231.0	$264.4
NET INTEREST	$ 85.2	$108.2	$116.1
General Gov't Bureaucracy	$ 19.1	$ 24.2	$ 27.7
Agriculture & Rural	$ 25.2	$ 14.0	$ 17.5
Public Infrastructure	$ 23.1	$ 26.2	$ 28.1
Security Assistance: Development Aid, Space & Other Defense	$ 22.4	$ 27.3	$ 33.0
TOTAL PAYMENTS	$796.0	$853.8	$925.5
DEFICIT	-$195.4	-$183.7	-$180.4

The one true purpose of taxation is to supply money with which to operate the government. There should be no favoritism, but there is. In one way or another wealthy people enjoy tax advantages. Some pay no taxes.

In 1913, the year the 16th amendment taxing incomes was added to the *Constitution,* wealthy men saw to it that Congress created loopholes for them. State, county and city bonds, called municipal bonds, were added to the then tax-free United States bonds. U.S. bonds were not taxed by the federal government until 1941. They remain untaxed by the states. (Most of these U.S. bonds are in financial institutions or foundations and therefore still free from most taxes.) Municipal bonds remain free from federal taxes and are tax-free in most states of issue.

There are now large amounts of other U.S. guaranteed bonds, such as housing bonds, that are tax-free. A recent report from fifty companies that manage money states that they handle some $365 billion in tax-free bonds. These tax-exempt bonds carry a slightly lower than usual interest rate. This differential cancels out when an income reaches $60,000. From there, as the income increases, the bonds are a bonanza. What counts is that their return does not push an income into higher tax brackets. Income from these bonds may be kept unreported and untaxed even if it runs into millions of dollars.

These things have not just happened. Financiers and their experts are always scheming and planning moves by the government which will protect their wealth and increase it.

There was never a true reason why the United States should have printed a single U.S. bond. If the truth were known, it is more than likely that as the outflow of municipal bonds lessened, the entire housing fiasco was inaugurated to provide these housing bonds as a tax-exempt haven for the wealthy. On May 7, 1981, the interest on government-guaranteed housing bonds was raised to 15.5 percent.

To pay political debts, and to further ingratiate themselves with those who might contribute again, Presidents and congressmen have, over the years, granted many tax favors. Most of these laws have remained on the books, and, together with new ones continually being added, make up the near 7,000 pages of the tax code.

The Internal Revenue Service, under pressure from politicians, writes many letters of tax favors. One example of such a letter is the Starker real estate exchange letter, number 7,938,087. The usual requirement for a tax-free sale and purchase of like property is that the replacement shall be present at time of sale. The Starkey letter provided that in that case the money from sale could be placed in escrow until a suitable replacement could be found.

Since newspapers published this the IRS has written another letter to the effect that the agency, the IRS, will decide in each case whether this rule applies.

Tax experts who serve the wealthy know all the tax shelters. They provide the wealthy with private trusts so that their income will be divided for a lower rate, and so that a large part of it may be paid to their children. The experts provide secret corporations. They know just how to avoid taxes on foreign incomes; how to stash funds in secret accounts in foreign banks. If there is no needed shelter they will try to get a law passed that will provide one.

Our wealthy internationalists, operating abroad, receive every consideration from our tax department. They also receive many leniencies from foreign governments in exchange for U.S. government grants to their nationals.

As an example of this last: an alien may escape Capital Gains Taxation if he makes a profit on sales or exchange of capital assets while in America under 183 days. However, since 1982, should he die and leave an estate of $60,000 or more, his heirs must file with the IRS.

Profits to our own citizens from the sale of investment property held for one year or longer is termed Long-Term Capital Gain. Its maximum federal tax is 20 percent.

For stockbrokers and other large traders having large profits and quick turnover, this provision is very helpful. That part of their income is separated from the rest and has a lower tax rate. Also it does not raise other income into higher tax brackets, which would run up to 50 percent.

As long ago as March 2, 1964, then Senator Walter Mondale said that 402 Americans with reportable incomes of more than $100,000 *paid no federal tax;* and that 99 of these had incomes of over $200,000 and that four had incomes of over $1 million for the year. Senator Mondale said that 624 Americans had incomes of over a million dollars and that many of these and thousands of other wealthy Americans ended up paying only a few hundred or a few thousand dollars in taxes — enough to keep their names off the list.

That the favored can arrange their affairs to pay as little tax as they like, or none, is shown by the fact that Nelson Rockefeller paid not a cent of taxes on one year, when his income was two and a half million dollars.

The Spotlight (6/7/82) states that Nelson Bunker Hunt, head of one of the nation's wealthiest families (worth some eight billion dollars), and his wife reported gross income of about $112 million for the three years 1975-1977, and paid a total federal income tax of $9.65.

The wealthy know how to pass most of their estates to their children. Many avoid an estate tax by putting their fortunes into foundations.

High estate and inheritance taxes absorb most ordinary estates in two generations. It would seem that great fortunes would be broken up, but they are not.

By the same token it seems that the U.S. bonds debt would have been greatly reduced — but no. Most bonds are held in corporations and foundations which do not die. These soulless, man-made fabrications are given rights denied the living.

To continue the picture; there were in the United States, as of December 31, 1977, over 800,000 organizations that were exempt from taxes.

The Other Side of the Coin

There is an old adage that the power to tax carries with it the power to destroy. Our officials in Washington seem utterly insensitive to the deadening effect of the tax burden they place on the middle class. They think and say that the government is losing so many millions or billions of dollars a year because it is not taxing something or other. They act as if every dollar taxpayers can get belongs to them to pay political debts, to operate the government, and to scatter on any pork barrel project that might bring votes.

Representative Al Ullman and Senator Russell Long did their best to fasten the nefarious, open-ended Added Value Tax upon us.

The word "reform" properly means to improve, to make better. In tax parlance it is used as a cloak for evil. Every tax reform adds to our burden. Step by step the trend is always upward.

According to *U.S. News & World Report* (6/29/81) federal taxes arose 85 percent in the previous five years.

The increase in Social Security taxes shocked the nation.

For the man in ordinary circumstances the 1040 form tells the story. He may search through the tax code and find nothing but sorrow for himself. Recently several 1040 tax credits have been lowered. The yearly inflation rate pushes up a worker's cost of living and his wages. This puts him into a higher tax bracket. With the "bracket creep" he is worse off than before. Paul Harvey told of one man who received a seven-percent raise in wages. This put him into a 24-percent higher income tax bracket. It is estimated that bracket creep cost taxpayers an extra $9 billion in 1980.

As mentioned earlier, the holding time for property to qualify for long-term capital gain tax exemption is one year.

There is no further exemption for property held longer. For property bought with very dear money some 20 to 50 years ago, a sale for today's depreciated money produces not a profit but a severe loss. There is first the selling commission of from six to ten percent for real estate, and 20 percent upward for fine antiques and works of art. Then comes the federal long-term capital gains tax which, even with exemptions, may be as much as 20 percent of the net profit. There is also, in most states, a state sales tax on the entire net book profit.

A seller of such property cannot take the remaining money and buy different property which is much more than half as good. Taxes on such sales are in restraint of trade. Few owners of such property will sell unless forced to do so.

This tax could be made more equitable if there were federal and state laws granting an exemption of the inflation rate, or if only five percent for the first year, and five percent for each year thereafter until a tax-free position is reached. This would encourage trade and bring more money into the treasury. But no. The long-term tax exemption was not devised for the average citizen. It was made for deals in stocks.

President Reagan's Tax Cut

A new tax bill was signed into law the middle of August 1981. There are some concessions — not near enough to counter recent inflation, to say nothing of the inflation to come in the five years before the bill is to be fully implemented.

As Sylvia Porter has said, this tax code is so mixed up and confusing that few can understand it. It will keep tax lawyers and accountants busy. The following seems clear.

There is now a percentage-wise tax cut across the board, with large savings for those with large incomes and little savings for those with little incomes. President Reagan justifies this by saying those who have large incomes save more than those with little. He wants to provide them with money — "supply-side" — "so they can invest and create jobs."

The tax bill greatly favors great corporations and individuals in high tax brackets. For those with large incomes there is the general tax cut and also the provision that the now maximum tax of 70 percent is reduced to 50 percent, and maximum estate tax is lowered from 70 to 50 percent — both gradually over the years until 1987.

(Right, but where are the little folks?)

We were told that there was a flood of telephone calls and letters approving President Reagan's tax cut bill — that messages approving ran twenty to thirty or more to one against it. This indicated, it was claimed, that a majority of our citizens favored the bill. It is likely that if a list was taken it would show that those who gave their approval were those who always call on the government to look after their interest. These are the wealthy individuals who give the $1000-a-plate political dinners and make political donations, and they are the great corporations which, through their Political Action Groups, elect congressmen and supply them with money. These are the ones who will receive most from the tax cuts.

Oil companies will receive all benefits given to other corporations and in addition will be allowed to keep, over the next ten years, $47 billion of the windfall tax money. Exxon, which had a 77-percent increase in profits for the second quarter of 1981, sent in its approval. On the NBC newscast, July 30, 1981, there was shown a copy of Exxon's letter urging congressmen to vote for the tax bill.

The 200,000,000 American citizens who individually will receive little from the tax cut were not heard from.

In a moment of candor Budget Director David Stockman spoke of President Reagan's three-year tax cut. He said that the worn out "trickle down" theory, that if the rich can be made rich enough some of the wealth may trickle down to the poor, would have been hard to sell to the

American people, and therefore the term "supply-side," was concocted. "Supply-side means trickle-down," he said, and was used as a Trojan horse to lower taxes for the wealthy.

The yearly tax-free gift to any one person has been raised from $3,000 to $10,000. This does not keep up with inflation which has, during the same time, priced property ten, twenty, or more times higher.

Cumulative transfers of estate which are to be free of inheritance taxes have been increased to $325,000 in 1984 and were to rise to $400,000 in 1985; $500,000 in 1986; $600,000 in 1987 and thereafter. However, President Reagan is now talking about "delay" of even this relief in the scramble to appease voter resistance to current deficit spending.

Even these figures, seemingly large, are not enough to offset inflation and high appraisals. Many properties, bought with very dear money 50 years ago, then permitted to be left to heirs without tax, are now subject to ruinous estate and inheritance taxes.

In those few cases where estate taxes are deferred, the tax still hangs over the property as a lien. Said Congressman James G. Martin (R-NC): "What the increased exemptions give the farmer today, the cost basis will take away tomorrow. The family owning a small farm or business has only a few years of grace."

It is a misuse of the taxing power to use it as an aid in regulating the economy — that is, increasing taxes at the appearance of good times. (They never really come down.) In a free-market economy there should be no excessive taxation.

It is also a serious injustice to use the taxing power to take earnings and savings of the middle class for distribution to others — above and below.

In November 1982, as our economy went from bad to worse, President Reagan proposed that those people in high tax brackets be given a Christmas present by moving up their July tax cut to January.

As of February 1983, a little after President Reagan's tax cut, he has signed into law a $98.3 billion tax increase on tobacco, telephones and the like. He has also signed into law a five-cent-a-gallon tax on gasoline and a large advance in taxes on truckers' licenses. All of these taxes will come, mainly, out of the middle economic class.

Instead of a real reform we are offered "Supply-Side Economy," which funnels money to the men who created our welfare state, and profit by it, and "Federalism." The latter is right in itself, but under present conditions would shift the care and support of the unemployed and destitute, mainly created by the bankers, onto the backs of local property owners.

Demands from a wildly extravagant Congress that the Internal Revenue Service keep its coffers full, countered by a rebellious spirit of many taxpayers, has led to a strange and sad change in equity. In April 1977 the United States Supreme Court ruled that Article 7, of the *U.S. Constitution* Bill of Rights, which provides for a jury trial before a citizen can be legally deprived of his property, is out of date and cannot be invoked in a dispute with the Internal Revenue Service. (It is claimed that this is necessary to keep courts from being swamped.)

The Internal Revenue Service makes its own rules and enforces them. It garnishes wages, empties bank accounts, padlocks businesses and seizes and sells delinquent taxpayers' property.

Taxation, to most of us, has become a dread affair.

Federal and state taxes are not our only tax problems. In Buncombe County, North Carolina, in March of 1982, there was a reassessment of property for tax purposes. The people, struggling to pay present taxes, were dismayed. On television were seen halls full of people making their ineffectual protest. The assessed value of some property was increased 800 percent. There will be a reduction in rate, but not enough to keep this property from a large increase in taxes.

Our last word here was said a century ago: "Unnecessary taxation is unjust taxation" (Abram S. Hewett, 1884).

It follows that most taxes are unjust for, as we shall see, most are unnecessary.

CHAPTER 12

Corporate Taxes

Many giant corporations with fabulous incomes pay little or no taxes.

In 1974 the windfall tax of some $13 or $14 billion on the oil companies was to carry a plow-back feature. If the companies would spend the money for new development, they would not be required to pay the tax. In short, our officials offered this tax as a plum when deregulating the price of oil, but at the same time, provided that it would never be collected.

In 1974 interest and inflation were increasing. On a newscast for November 25 that year, the extent of unemployment was reported. It too was steadily increasing. The automobile manufacturers had laid off some 200,000 workers. Manufacturing plants throughout the nation were curtailing production; many were closing. Secretary Simon's image came upon the screen. To dampen the economy he was in favor of a raise in taxes. "But not," he said, "on corporations. They need the money to reinvest."

The Asheville Citizen-Times (6/29/80) quotes Rep. Charles A. Vanik (D-OH), as saying that 14 companies earning more than $3.5 billion among them paid no federal income tax in 1978, and another 30 earning $14.4 billion paid less than 10 percent to the government. A number of banks paid an average of 6.3 percent on $19.9 billion income.

While corporations are busy adding estimated taxes to the price of their products, their attorneys are busy conjuring up every possible device to keep from passing the money to the U.S. Treasury. An interesting help for this is furnished by the so-called "Safe Harbor," tax break to corporations, passed into law in 1981.

This law allows a corporation to sell a plant or equipment, and then rent it. The purchaser may take large tax depreciations on the property and, if this tax credit is not needed, sell it to the first company. (This must have been dreamed up by company lobbyists.) It is unlikely that there has been any reduction in prices that were added to pay these now-forgiven taxes.

A good article on this may be read in the *U.S. News & World Report* for November 23, 1981, which quotes Senator Dale Bumpers (D-AR) as saying: "It basically repeals the corporate income tax."

It has been estimated that in 1982, the federal taxes collected from corporations amounted to only eight percent of the whole.

Senator Howard Metzenbaum (D-OH) has said that in fiscal year 1983, we would give $295 billion in tax subsidies to corporations; that this is more than corporations pay in federal income tax. The Bank of America, Dow Chemical, Union Pacific and Tenneco are among those corporations which, in 1981, did not pay one dime in corporate income tax.

No one can say whether a particular corporation owes taxes, and really what difference does it make? There is no way these corporations can be forced to pay (from themselves) a federal tax. All such assessments must be added by them to the price of their product, and passed on to their customers — many of whom are least able to pay. Then too, the tax money paid in this way passes through a complex tax system where much of it is dissipated in the handling. We should search for a better way of handling this.

CHAPTER 13

Foundations

There is a general belief that when owners of great fortunes die, their holdings are broken up by estate taxes. Nothing could be further from the truth. Typical of such arrangements is the following account:

After giving his sons enormous fortunes, one wealthy man left an estate of $200 million dollars. One-half went tax free to his widow through marital deduction. The other $100 million went into a foundation. There was no inheritance tax. The family of the founder usually controls the foundation, and selects its managers. The foundation owns the stock that made the fortune, and thus keeps control of the foundation in the family. *The Christian Science Monitor* (10/25/72) quoted from the "20th Century Fund": "Not one-tenth, probably not one-twentieth, of their grants have any measurable impact upon the major social problems confronting the nation at the present time." *The Christian Science Monitor* goes on to state "The programs many foundations support are intellectually fraudulent or petty."

It is true that these foundations endow chairs in universities. It is also true that many students come from those universities imbued with the tenets of these foundations. That seems to be the purpose of the grants. Many foundations simply meddle, searching for ways to justify their operators' salaries. Some have engaged in foreign intrigue. Some attempt to force the view of their originators, long dead, on society. Some spend large amounts in their efforts to force acceptance of their present holder's philosophy.

It is charged that some foundations did some good at their beginning, but then came under control of men bent on breaking down the autonomy of the United States, and carrying it into a world government. And further, that in this attempt, their actions have had a serious, destructive influence on our national sense of unity; love for our country; our home life; our educational system; and our religions. Deliberate or not, there is ample proof that foundations have spent many millions of tax-free dollars on various studies and projects that have these effects. It is charged that much of the present-day pornography and decline of morals can be traced to the foundation-sponsored Kinsey Report.

Other foundations, operating under the banner of "Education," have financed the takeover of school systems. Subversive, filthy textbooks have been introduced into public schools. Protesting parents have been overruled. Basic education has given way to sociology. Many high school graduates have not mastered simple arithmetic, cannot read and understand an average printed page. And now, instead of honest, earnest attempts being made to sharpen their ability — the majestic, beautiful, spiritual King James Version of the Bible has been traded for versions brought down to their level. The new Bibles are commonplace in comparison with the old. Some contain words not used in polite discourse. The declining effects of these things are felt in the lives of us all.

To avoid the confiscatory estate tax of that day, Henry

Ford established the Ford Foundation in 1936. He gave the foundation 80 percent of the Ford Motor Company in Class B non-voting stock. The stated purpose of the foundation was to "Advance human welfare," chiefly through educational grants. The Foundation's assets as of 1975 were $2,070,228,000. Its income is a share of Ford Motor Company profits.

The Ford Foundation is an example of a foundation that has been taken over by men of very different philosophy from its founder. The men who control this large amount of money did not earn it, but they handle it as their own.

In a twelve-page reprint, "Tax-Free Cash," from *American Opinion* (November 1968), Harold Varner charged that the Ford Foundation with some $3.19 billion in assets has debased America. His scathing denunciation will not be repeated here.

It has been thirteen years since that article was written. Recently the present Henry Ford wrote the Foundation's Director a chilling letter and resigned from the foundation his grandfather had established.

Time (11/28/80) showed a picture of a handsome 36-story building on 5th Avenue at 52nd Street, New York. It was formerly owned by the Iranian Shah; now it is owned by the tax-free Pahlavi Foundation. Foreign tax-free foundations must be scattered over the United States.

In 1935 John D. McArthur bought Bankers' Life and Casualty Company of Chicago for a trifle. This company appealed to the little man, the poor and the aged.

Mr. McArthur became a billionaire; he died January 6, 1978. He left his fortune in a tax-free foundation without a word as to how it is to be used. The way the foundation's annual income of perhaps $40 million is spent is left, mainly, to Mr. McArthur's insurance associates.

The apparent reason for this foundation — like most

others — was to avoid the estate tax.

Due to the tax-free status of foundations and to other generous exemptions of some businesses, airlines and other institutions, as well as churches, schools and businesses run by these, it is estimated that about one-third of the property of the nation is not assessed for a local property tax. In New York nearly half of the visible property is not taxed; in Newark, about half; in Boston, 54 percent is exempt. Since 1969 foundations operating as charitable, scientific, prevention of cruelty to animals, educational and religious, pay no property tax. The number of tax-free foundations in the United States is estimated to be at least 31,000.

CHAPTER 14

"Free Trade" or National Suicide?

In early autumn of 1979 President Carter went to Europe to sign a free trade agreement. This opened the way for General Motors to finalize their plan to build cars abroad and bring them into the United States. Almost immediately after the signing, General Motors, laying off tens of thousands of workers here, announced that it would, at the cost of $2 billion, build a factory in Austria to make engines, and build two factories in Spain to make cars and parts. The Spanish factories would employ at least 10,000 workers.

Since then it has transpired that General Motors is having cars built in Japan and Brazil. Parts of Ford's "world" cars are built in many foreign countries.

Great corporations that have swallowed other corporations are closing their factories in the United States and are building in foreign lands where they can be free from our labor unions, employ cheaper labor and better conceal profits. Their products are brought into this country for sale to those they will not employ.

Treaty or no treaty, most foreign countries do not admit

our goods as we admit theirs. Japanese manufacturers sell cars in the United States at lower prices than they set in Japan. Japanese regulations and their system of inspection rule out most of our exports. It has been reported that after conforming to these regulations an American car selling for $8,000 in the United States sells for $26,000 in Japan!

"Free trade" is not so much to sell American goods, or yet bring in foreign goods, as it is to give our internationalists a free hand to operate abroad — to open banks there, and to manufacture goods there — for sale abroad and to bring into this country, duty-free.

Financiers, having gained ownership of most of the profitable productive property of this nation and legal claims (bonds) for most of the remainder; having control of those who control the police and Army to enforce these claims; and having had the Presidents enter into a great many treaties with foreign nations, have lost much of their enthusiasm for the United States of America. They are turning their attention to new fields in foreign lands.

(There is some justification for this search for "greener fields." Here in the United States the courts and labor unions tell them who to employ, who to promote and what to pay. The bureaucrats plague them with thousands of senseless regulations and reports.)

Using America as a sound base, these internationals have formed multinational corporations, and, carrying American wealth, technology and machinery with them, have established factories and outlets all over the world.

Thus, while American automobile corporations were bringing in thousands of cars made in their foreign plants, they were laying off tens of thousands of their American workers.

The Charlotte Observer (6/3/82) under the caption, "Business Creates Welfare State," tells of Mary McDaniels, a Hotpoint Electric iron worker.

"She lost an income of more than $400 a week because G.E. can get someone in Singapore to do what she was doing for $45 a week."

Needless to say, the irons, when brought into this country, are not reduced a corresponding amount in price.

These foreign factories and enterprises are largely unregulated and untaxed, as far as the United States is concerned.

In mid-September 1983, it was announced that Warner Communications Corporation will move its California plant to Hong Kong and Taiwan for cheaper labor, idling 7,000 American laborers.

For American corporations to bring in, duty-free, goods cheaply made in their foreign factories, and to sell at the old price, must be extremely profitable. Yet, year after year, these corporations report great losses. How can they stay in business?

They must mean losses through their weird bookkeeping on operations here.

Our financiers' foreign operations are secret. They pay no American tax on them. It could be that on their foreign factory books they charge so much for parts going to their American assembly line that the American factory is made to show a large loss. This book loss can be well used. Through the "Safe Harbor" provision this tax-credit can be sold to another American factory, owned by the same financiers. This factory, which would otherwise show a profit, also comes out tax-free.

Countries in need must offer concessions to entice our financiers to build factories on their soil. This opens the way for citizens of other industrialized nations to claim such rights here. This nation is filling up with foreign-owned factories, mixing our economy with all others. American-owned factories are overseas; foreign-owned factories are in America.

This nation is not a solid nation, operating for the good of all its inhabitants. The internationalists have all but destroyed its unity. What will happen in the case of war?

Having surrendered our markets for the export of manufactured goods, this nation attempts to balance its foreign trade by exporting raw products such as food, as well as arms.

This foreign trend has weakened the United States and strengthened our rivals. It is said that everything the Soviets have was carried to them from the West.

The United States gave; the Soviets acceded with platitudes which were then disregarded. The Helsinki Agreement, wherein the United States acknowledged the right of Russia to enslave millions of East Europeans, was this and nothing more.

The huge Kama River Truck factory in the Soviet Union — the largest in the world — covers more than 38 square miles and will employ some 90,000 people. American companies put up four billion dollars to build the plant. *Red Star,* the Soviet army newspaper, showed illustrations of enormous trucks bristling with deadly missiles.

If a profit is made, the financiers take it. If a loss is shown, it is assumed by the American people. It is now estimated that Soviet debts to the West total about $71 billion, and the banks are looking to the American taxpayer to pay it.

In telling how our great bankers built Russia at the expense of the United States, Alexsandr Solzhenitsyn said: "This is something almost incomprehensible to the human mind: that burning greed for profit which goes beyond all reason, all self-control, all conscience, only to get money."

We quote from a letter, signed Theodore S. Brandwein

in the *Miami Herald,* January 6, 1974, "So that a few self-interested corporate giants can further enrich themselves, the American public is being called upon to encourage and finance the economic expansion of the Soviet Union."

And now it seems, the same line is to be followed in China. The talk of great markets awaiting us there — the selling of trucks, farm machinery and the like — was set straight on a newscast February 10, 1979. The Chinese do not want to buy these things. They want the United States to provide factories so they can make these trucks and implements for themselves — and, of course, to sell to us. That vast country has a billion intelligent, industrious people. Life and labor is cheap. Given financial backing, our most efficient machines, computers, and know-how, China would flood this nation with goods, and underselling, take our foreign markets, putting our laborers out of work.

It is proposed that we arm China. To arm this vast communistic country would be extremely dangerous. A nation that would kill 64 million of its own dissenters would not hesitate to kill dissenters in other countries. We should note how rapidly Red China's friendship for us waned when we sought to honor our mutual defense treaty with Taiwan.

At the slightest disagreement, or chance for advancement, a country which has received our arms may use them against us, or else, joining the Soviets, give them, to copy our latest and most sophisticated weapons.

CHAPTER 15

Boring From Within

It is clear that the internationalists, through their control of our monetary system, have gained control of our central government and most of the nation's wealth and natural resources; and using our government as a lever, have spread their operations over the world. These things, all so evident, are not, however, the main point — the main danger here. This nation, the United States of America, as designed and left to us by our forefathers, and loved by most of our people, does not suit the fancy and the purpose of the internationalists. They are citizens of the world.

Boring from within, striking down all opposition with their massive bank roll, a mere handful of men, bent on further personal gain and power, are attempting to break down the identity and independence of our nation and internationalize it.

All Southern Florida has changed. Miami has only 15 percent of white people — the people who made the city. The American taxpayer is required to support millions of aliens and educate their children. Some city schools are required to teach their classes in Spanish.

Despite the lessons of what eventually happens in a nation made up of many strong diverse factions (races, religions, customs) as seen in Lebanon and many other places, the mixing continues here.

The United States-Mexico border is 2,000 miles long. It has been patrolled by 2,300 guards. Their call for help has been ignored. Said one guard, "It seems as if the government wants these Mexicans to come in." Millions do pour in and go on relief. All Southern California is growing dark. Many aliens take jobs from Americans. And, upon nationalization, these aliens will come under the present employment quota system, and the chances of our natives getting a job will be ever smaller.

Our citizens must endure aliens' crime and dreadful diseases. Our prisons and hospitals are filling up with them.

No nation can continue to exist under such circumstances as have been placed on this nation. Other nations fiercely guard their identity. Neither Russia nor any other country is thought less of for maintaining control of its borders. It is only in the United States that such destructive manipulations are allowed. In the summer of 1983 Brazil began the expulsion of 700,000 illegal aliens from surrounding countries.

Yet our government makes citizens of these, splintering and impoverishing the nation, and raises taxes to supply them with welfare checks. The President, uneasy that the old citizens will not vote for him in the next election, appeals to the newcomers for their votes.

For the meaning of it all my mind goes back to Ronald Reagan's statement immediately after the internationalists endorsed him for office. On his recent trip through South and Central America his pointed and oft-repeated call for unity caused a reporter of the *U.S. News & World Report* to ask if the President was contemplating the forging of the nations of the Western Hemisphere into a United States of the Americas.

Having joined with the wealthiest men of other lands, our great financiers are edging closer to their goal.

They would have us believe that they have the money, technology, and intelligence to manage the world as an integrated unit. The question is, are these the kind of men we want to rule us, in a world government which would end all our freedom?

Most of their corporations became great through special privileges gained by bribery, by price rigging, falsification of reports, theft of millions of tons of grain entrusted to their ships, income tax evasion, confusing deals with their own secret corporations, their weird bookkeeping, the surrounding and capture of other companies and loot of their assets. In search of the last possible dollar of profit, with no regard to its effect on the nation, these men have moved their factories overseas, and to bring in their own foreign goods, duty-free, have flooded this nation with other foreign goods. Our nation is sinking in unemployment and debt.

In considering the role of the Council on Foreign Relations, the Bilderbergers, the Trilateral Commission and the Club of Rome, one thing stands out and is certain: the primary blame for the rapid decline of this nation from its abundance and its position as the supreme world power may be laid directly upon the leaders of the internationalists who have controlled our government and economy.

The Men Who Make the Rules

The "President's Executive Interchange Program" was established in 1969. Under this program the government, on a yearly exchange basis, may bring as many as 50 high executives from giant corporate board rooms into government conference rooms. These men assist in formulating policies and rules for the regulation and control of their own industries and utilities.

It has been charged that the plan is largely political. Those making the largest contributions get assignments that, to them, mean the most.

These men bring with them mastery of their subjects; prestige of their corporate positions; and always the possibility that they may hand out a lucrative job as reward to any government worker who goes along with a ruling favorable to their corporations. The policies of these men are tainted with self-protection, and with the desire for larger profit. Jack Anderson cited one incident in 1975 in which the cost may have been as much as $100 million.

The cover of *U.S. News & World Report* for September 6, 1982, shows a picture of a board room and carries in large letters the words: CORPORATE CRIME. The story states that in the last ten years there have been at least 2690 corporations convicted of crime. This includes 115 of America's largest corporations; a number of others have pled no contest. Consumer advocates estimate that the cost to the nation is as much as $200 billion a year.

Some of these crimes are blamed on managers. "In other instances, criminal conspiracies are masterminded by the very top officers of the firm."

For only one of a number of such reports, read "Bribery Is Bad Business," by Irwin Ross in November, 1976, *Readers' Digest*. He tells how U.S. multinationals have handed out millions of dollars in bribes. Out of some 175 companies reporting their bribery, 117 are among the largest and supposedly the most ethical corporations in the United States.

Through their control of our economy and our government these men could have led this nation into an era of prosperity and safety such as the world has never known. What an opportunity for nobility! Instead, the demand has always been for personal profit and further expansion of their global interests, regardless of the damage to the nation and destruction of its middle class.

These men can never, personally, use more than a tiny fraction of the wealth they now hold. What is their real purpose? Is it greed alone, or is it, as some writers have warned: overriding ambition, and a relentless, ruthless, dangerous drive for power?

We are told that if great corporations are made rich enough, there will be many more jobs and prosperity for all.

Yet creating jobs and general prosperity are not the chief aims of great corporations. Corporations are out for profit, and, in manufacturing this is derived from the cheapest possible labor. One way to obtain this is through automation.

Industrialists say they want to invest $3 billion in modernizing their factories. In Japan one whole factory is run entirely by robots — making more robots. Only 100 people come in for eight hours to see that everything is going well.

There are an estimated 15,000 robots in the United States.

One robot can do the work of five men, and do it better.

On October 30, 1981, an Asheville newscast stated that the American Enka plant was to discharge 115 workers. An official of the company was asked if they would be rehired. He replied that some of the jobs would be taken over by automation. This is what the great corporations mean by modernization. Automation, we are told, will relieve people of tedious and dangerous jobs. Under present conditions it will also take away their means of making a living.

Another way of obtaining cheap labor is to move factories from the United States to foreign lands where labor is cheap. This is continuing at a rapid pace.

President Reagan has said nothing about controlling great corporations which hold, and by mergers are increasing, their monopolies on food and other necessities of life, and are forever raising prices. There could be cheaper labor here if unconscionable profiteering were controlled. This cannot be done by increasing corporate taxation. The cost of taxes would be added to the prices.

Yet in a Washington speech the middle of May, 1982, President Reagan expressed concern over the burgeoning welfare state, due in no small part to multinational industry moves overseas.

"In 1950 social programs cost taxpayers $12 billion, in 1980 nearly $300 billion.

"Sixteen years ago we were spending 65 million dollars on food stamps — sixty-five million. In 1981 we spent 11.3 billion dollars. That's an increase of over 16,000 percent."

CHAPTER 16

Internationalism

The first great threat to the continuity of our republican form of government came soon after World War I. President Woodrow Wilson, chosen and financed by internationalists, with "Colonel" E.M. House by his side, toured our nation, speaking from the rear platform of his private train, attempting to carry our nation into a League of Nations. The fact that Woodrow Wilson had been elected to preserve the government of this nation, and had sworn to abide by its *Constitution* made no difference to him. The Senate insisted upon retention of the constitutional provision that only Congress, and not the League of Nations, could commit this nation to war, and the internationalist scheme fell through.

Before the end of the Second World War the idea surfaced again. This time it was not so overt.

In 1944 a "United Nations Monetary and Financial Conference" was held in Bretton Woods, New Hampshire. Details on this matter are in my other book, *Honest Money*. Suffice it to say here that CFR member Harry Dexter White architected that conference and the International Monetary

Fund (IMF) and World Bank born then. The purpose of these organizations was to facilitate the massive transfer of wealth from the United States to communist nations and the Third World which has been occurring ever since. The conference also paved the way for the U.N., formed a year later. Here are the goals of its major organizations designed to further economic internationalism:

1. The International Monetary Fund. Its stated purpose is to promote monetary cooperation and currency stability. It is to this fund that President Reagan promised $50 billion ($8.4 of this has been approved by Congress). The money is loaned by the bankers to debtor countries to pay the interest on their defaulting loans.

2. The International Bank for Reconstruction and Development (World Bank). This bank is supposed to assist backward countries in their development. It provides that to its funds other funds may be added from private investors, who then share in the project. We all know what that means. It means that those who put in the extra money, the bankers, will control the project and reap a lion's share, or all of any profits.

3. International Finance Corporation. This bank is to promote the private sector in foreign countries, and providing loans to develop foreign markets. Overseeing the distribution of these funds, the international bankers may, to curry favor, see that money is loaned to foreign rulers, and enter a country with their own banks and businesses. (It is reported that the Chase-Manhattan bank has branch banks in 125 countries.) As for developing markets, this bank may make loans to foreigners, providing them with money to pay for goods from the banker's factories, both here and in foreign countries.

These organizations have made possible the dominance of world trade by multinational corporations since the end of

World War II. According to the London *Economist* (4/21/79) multinationals are "companies with assets in more than one country."

An excellent article on multinationals appeared in *Forbes Magazine* (6/25/79). A quote there from G.A. Costanzo of Citicorp, largest U.S. multinational bank, should help the reader to understand the rationale of those who want to deindustrialize America and bring her to ruin.

"In 1958 we may have thought that we could get our overseas earnings up from 5% or 10% of our total earnings to maybe 20%. But I doubt if in our wildest imagination we thought it would ever be more than 50-50. Now we're at 80-20."

In the past 30 years our internationalists joined forces with foreign internationalists and really went multinational. These have been the years of the great bankers' rigamarole about government borrowing (which they forced), creating the necessity for high interest rates, the years when these bankers carried their branch banks, and scattered the resources of this country over the world. These are the years our major industrialists searched for cheaper labor, not to reduce prices, but for more profit, discharging millions of their workers here and moving their factories to foreign lands. These are the years that owners of great corporations, to curry favor abroad and to bring in the product of their foreign factories, had our government pass one-sided laws and treaties for free trade, which permitted them and foreigners to flood this country with foreign goods.

The following is quoted from a letter of Billy J. Harris, in the *U.S. News & World Report,* December 4, 1978.

"I went shopping with my daughter today. She bought a pair of shoes from Italy, two blouses from Japan, a belt from Hong Kong and two skirts made in Korea. She bought for style, workmanship and price. We could not find American-made goods that compare."

In the summer of 1982 I received a present of a nice traveling bag. It was made in Korea. And then a pair of headphones — from Korea. For Christmas 1983, it was an automatic telephone caller from Taiwan, and timer from Hong Kong.

Most television sets, an increasing number of automobiles, motorcycles, bicycles, cameras, typewriters, electronics, toys, are made abroad.

All large printing presses and much of the great modern machines for our large manufacturing plants are shipped in. If an item is labeled "made in U.S.A.," it often means that it was assembled here from foreign-made parts.

Our workmen who once made these things are idle — subsisting on what remains of the savings of our economic middle class.

Our internationalists have made Japan a great industrialized nation. They have made the United States of America a supplier of raw products. Even copper ore, mined in America, is sent to Japan to be smelted. The difference lies in the nature and character of the men in charge of the two nations. The Japanese overlords are all for a world government — for us, but not for Japan. The immensely wealthy men who control our government and economy are bent on destroying the unity and integrity of this country and bringing it into their planned "New World Order."

That internationalism is killing American free enterprise, the goose that laid the golden egg, is evident from the November 1980 Special Report #9 of the Public Policy Education Fund at Grove City College in Pennsylvania. Professor John A. Sparks wrote that of the 156 largest companies in the world, 111 or 71 percent were U.S. multinationals in 1959. "By 1976, U.S. companies made up a much smaller 44 percent of the largest firms." Dr. Sparks said that of American investments overseas in 1980, 72 percent was in developed countries; 24 percent in the Third World; four percent unallocated.

The Sparks report on multinationals also gave a breakdown on U.S. investment in lesser developed countries: 17% "extractive" (6% mining and smelting; 11% petroleum); 35% manufacturing; 10% trade; finance and insurance 27%.

World Business Weekly (8/4/80) reported that industrialized countries increased their purchases of manufactured goods *from* the Third World an incredible 60% during the 1970's!

Even worse, "between 32 million and 38 million jobs were lost during the 1970's as the direct result of private *dis*investment in American business," said Barry Bluestone and Bennett Harrison in their powerful book, *The Deindustrialization of America,* published by Basic Books in 1982.

"Between 1950 and 1980, direct foreign investments by U.S. business increased 16 times from about $12 billion to $192 billion," said Bluestone and Harrison. "Every $1 billion of direct private U.S. foreign investment seems to eliminate . . . about 26,500 jobs. . . . Plant closings and other forms of disinvestment may be robbing the nation of $200 billion annually in foregone output, $60 billion in federal tax receipts, and forcing Americans to spend over $12 billion more each year in income assistance (unemployment compensation, then welfare and food stamps). This is obviously no small price to pay and these figures do *not* include foregone taxes and added expenses for *state* and *local* governments."

Is it any wonder that Japan, built by these Trilateral policies, has rushed into the economic vacuum here in America?

As of October 1982, Japan owned outright or partially 400 factories in the United States. It was announced on CBS, May 17, 1983, that there are 250 Japanese restaurants in New York, and that in New York there are 700 businesses doing a billion dollar business a month.

Recently a Japanese official said that if American workmen made as good automobiles as the Japanese make, the United States would not have to worry about imports.

American workmen, on the assembly line, must put in parts supplied to them. Many, perhaps most of these parts are made in foreign countries. Several years ago, perhaps as far back as 1975, a reliable car repair man tells me, alternators and starters, having American manufacturers' names cast on them, came in boxes having papers that stated the part was made in Japan.

Our Commerce Department analysts estimate that for the year 1984, our net foreign trade loss may be $100 billion.

The United Nations

In Moscow, October 19-30, 1943, the big four allied powers (UK, US, USSR, and Republic of China) agreed to form a united nations organization. At Yalta February 4-11, 1945, Churchill, Roosevelt, and Stalin agreed on voting arrangements for the forthcoming internationalist network. There would be an 11-member Security Council, with each of the big four plus France having veto power. Also, the Soviets insisted on three votes in the General Assembly, where all other nations have one vote each.

The United Nations began officially in San Francisco on June 26, 1945, when delegates of 50 nations signed the UN Charter. A month later it was ratified by the U.S. Senate, only two senators voting against it. One of these, Sen.

William Langer (R-ND) warned, "(The UN) is fraught with danger to the American people and to American institutions."

Russian-born Dr. Leo Pasvolsky headed the Special Division of the State Department that wrote the outline for the United Nations.

The Rockefellers (who gave the ground for the building) and other internationalists, including Alger Hiss (charged with supplying United States secrets to Russia before World War II and convicted of perjury; together with Russian agents and sympathizers) led the United States into this expensive and dangerous jungle.

The United Nations was not created for the unity, the preservation and benefit of our nation. Read its "Organization" in a *World Almanac*.

On one page of the "Organization," the word "international" is repeated 17 times.

The United Nations became an open door and a haven for spies.

It was reported that in the Korean and Vietnam wars our military were required to report battle plans to the United Nation's Department of Political and Security Affairs. The Under-Secretary who heads this department of the UN has always been a communist in the nearly forty years of its existence. Of the 13 who have held the post, 12 were Soviets; one a Yugoslav. Few Americans realize that in these no-win wars, our men were required to fight under a UN flag, reporting to these men. What this meant can be seen in the following words of General Lewis Walt, from his book, *The Eleventh Hour*.

"It bothered me deeply that I was required to submit 24 hours in advance a detailed plan of attack for approval by UN Command Headquarters. It bothered me because it soon became apparent that each time we attacked, the enemy was waiting for us. . . . We could not achieve surprise. We could not retain anything we won. . . . The Chinese fought under no UN restrictions."

At one time the Senate went so far as to pass a bill placing the United States under the United Nation's Court of Justice (world court). Total abdication of our nation's control of its foreign affairs, and many overlapping domestic ones, was prevented by Tom Connally's amendment of six words: "AS DETERMINED BY THE UNITED STATES." From time to time there have been efforts to repeal this amendment. In 1972 Hubert Humphrey, a member of the Council on Foreign Relations, and a man who came within an eyelash of the Presidency, sponsored such a bill.

On April 30, 1982, the United Nations passed a Law of the Sea Treaty — the United States abstaining. Under this treaty, with the exception of coastal waters, the entire sea, its shipping lanes, airplanes, fishes, oil, gas and metals pass to control of the U.N. The enormous wealth of minerals is to be placed under control of an International Sea Bed Authority. The industrial nations, meaning chiefly the United States, would be required to furnish the technique and money for the Authority. Our ships at present engaged in this would continue, but more is doubtful. They would be subject to restrictions as to how much they mined. Each ship would be charged a million dollars a year, and then "taxed" 70 percent of the value of their take — the money divided among the Third World Nations. The United States would have no voice or control. The Treaty could be changed and the screws further tightened by the Sea Bed officials — without our consent.

The United Nations' vague, ill-defined and dangerous Genocide Treaty has been brought up again and again.

Causing hurt feelings by a remark about a race is punishable under the Treaty. Apparently a Polish joke may be grounds for suit. But the major target of the Genocide Treaty is the person who would share his religion with others, making it a crime.

Under this treaty an American citizen might be accused, arrested by United Nations officials and tried before a foreign tribunal. If after his expenses and the ordeal he is found guilty, the punishment as laid down in the treaty, would be "effective penalties" which might mean anything. Under the treaty two members of any group could complain to the U.N. that they were mentally hurt by some action or word of some citizen. The United States courts could not protect him.

One must go back to the *Constitution* to realize the full meaning of such a treaty. ARTICLE VI states: "all treaties made or which shall be made, under the authority of the United States, shall be the supreme law of the land, and the judge in every State shall be bound thereby, anything in the *Constitution* or laws of any State to the contrary, notwithstanding."

The American Bar Association now joins the Third World nations, subversive groups, communists, internationalists, Chairman of the Foreign Relations' Committee Charles Percy, Senator William Proxmire and others who are in favor of this surrender of our sovereignty.

The United States hosts the United Nations. We did pay 40 percent of all its expenses here and abroad. We now pay 25 percent. The United States has only one vote among 156 — mostly hostile ones. A majority of voting members, taken together, pay only three percent of expenses.

Read "The U.N.: A Bureaucrat's Land of Milk and Honey," in *U.S. News & World Report,* for February 21, 1983. The salaries of these officials and delegates are very high. They live in luxury. There is never the slightest sign of appreciation or gratitude. Never has the United Nations contributed anything good to this country. It has been a sounding board to be used in criticizing and damning this country while protecting the atrocities of others.

Rose L. Martin exposes the United Nations in chapter five of *The Selling of America.*

A more recent denunciation is that of Jean Kirkpatrick, our present Ambassador to the United Nations. She denounced the United Nations as an expensive fraud, one that is anything but a peacemaker. Mrs. Kirkpatrick said: ''The UN now serves, not to settle conflict, but to polarize, extend and exacerbate it.''

The *U.S. News & World Report* of September 20, 1982, reports that Perez de Cueller, Secretary General of the United Nations, says that the United Nations cannot play an effectual role in settling world disputes. He names Afghanistan, Lebanon, Iran-Iraq, Falklands, and Cypress.

And now there is a strong campaign of 123 members advocating a redistribution of the wealth of Western industrial nations and giving it to undeveloped nations.

Over the earth there are some 40 wars now being fought.

A look at the United Nations gives a good idea of what a world government would be.

British Prime Minister Margaret Thatcher pointed out (6/82) that since 1945 there have been ''140 conflicts in which up to 10 million people have died.''

This was quoted in FAC-Sheet #36 of the Plymouth Rock Foundation, P.O. Box 425, Marlborough, NH 03455, which also gave the results of public opinion polls on the UN in America. ''In 1959, Gallup reported 87% of Americans thought UN was doing a good job. Since then, *public has lost confidence.* In 1970, 50% thought UN was effective . . . in 1980, 31% (with 53% saying *UN does poor job).* In 1981, a Roper poll found only *10%* thought UN effective. A 1983 survey found Americans highly critical of UN operations; negative opinions ran higher than 90%."

A recent ABC-TV poll revealed Americans want UN to leave the U.S., two to one! Finally the U.S. Senate voted (9/22/83) to cut U.S. contributions by 21 percent for fiscal 1983-84, and 10 percent more in each of the following three years.

Senator Jesse Helms (R-NC) has suggested that the UN move its headquarters to Moscow. If this is done and all U.S. financial support is cut off, with the U.S. withdrawing its membership, the whole Tower of Babel which has been at the root of much of our trouble will be gone. Also, the Reds will have lost a major propaganda base and spy base in the U.S.

Control of Thought

Through the years great bankers have bought up most of the large publishing houses. They have collected whole chains of newspapers.

Through it all the Federal Communications Commission has maintained a limit on the number of AM and FM radio stations and television stations that any one man, or any one company could own. The number has been seven of each. It is reported that President Reagan plans to scrap that regulation and allow unlimited acquisition.

Those men who now control the nation's government and economy control most of the nation's media.

According to the Council on Foreign Relations annual report for 1979-1980, 209 members are journalists, correspondents and communications executives.

The MacNeil-Lehrer Report co-produced by the WNET/THIRTEEN, New York and WETA/Washington

D.C., examines and discusses one story each night. It is a sample of what is to come.

It is financed by Exxon, the Bell System and member stations of PBS.

In *Time* for February 28, 1983, there is a full page advertisement calling upon the people to "Watch Reagan's New Federalism": Wednesday, March 2, at 9:00 p.m. on PBS.

The ad is made possible by a grant from the Getty Oil Company.

Great corporations are not the only ones to use force in an attempt to control thought. An article in *The Spotlight* names 23 liberal organizations whose members watch the trade journals for notice of sales of radio and television stations. The group then forms a committee, and threatens the management that it will file a petition to deny the sale unless it will sign a contract agreeing to all sorts of hiring practices, and to put designated programs on the air. Delay is costly and the management is forced to sign.

Most bookstores will not handle such a book as this one. They have no way of finding out about it, unless a customer makes a special request for it. Few Americans realize that book distribution is controlled by a handful of middle men who decide what they will market and offer the stores only what their owners approve. The best discounts go to those who buy all their titles, or most of them, from such suppliers. Naturally, approved titles follow the line of the major news media.

After we study the media chart of CFR-TC members at the end of chapter 2, we might well ask ourselves: Have we come to George Orwell's "Thought Police" in *1984?*

The Concentration of Wealth

With interest from trillions of dollars they have typed into their computers, and with dozens of laws giving them a free hand, a few financiers have made rapid progress in the last few years. They now own outright, or have claims to, most of the wealth of the nation.

We shall take a look, hardly more than a glance, at the details of the financiers' vast holdings, and then a glance at that left to the people.

Recently I was stopped at a grade crossing by a slowly passing freight train. On the locomotive was a placard stating that it was owned by a certain bank, and leased to the operating company. Each and every car of the long train bore such a placard.

The bankers own the giant airplanes that fly above us, and lease them to operating companies.

Banks own and lease computers — even those operated by many huge corporations.

The following is from the *Don Bell Report,* January 1, 1981.

"The list of corporations contained in this table of multiple interlocking directorates with the Rockefeller Family represents an immense portion of the entire economic apparatus of this country. This table includes 6 of the top 10 Industrial Corporations listed by *Fortune,* 6 of the top 10 Commercial Banking Corporations listed by *Fortune,* 5 of the top 10 Life Insurance Corporations listed by *Fortune,* and 2 or 3 of the top 10 corporations in the other four categories listed by *Fortune.* The combined assets of all the companies listed here add up to $640,000,000,000.

"Major Corporations Having Multiple Interlocks
With the Rockefeller Family

"*Industrials:* General Motors (2); Exxon (3); Chrysler (RF&A-1); General Electric (2); Mobil Oil

(3); IBM (RF&A+4); U.S. Steel (3); RCA (2); Eastman Kodak (2); Union Carbide (2); Caterpillar Tractor (2); Xerox (4); W.R. Grace (4); General Foods (5); Singer (2); Ralson Purina (2); Honeywell (2); Bendix (RF&A+2); Colgate-Palmolive (4); American Can (2); TRW (3); National Steel (3); Uniroyal (4); Republic Steel (2); American Motors (RF&A); FMC (2); Werner-Lambert (2); Allied Chemical (2); U.S. Industries (3); Raytheon (2); Eaton (2); Standard Oil, Ohio (2); Teledyne (2); Nabisco (2); Kennecott Copper (4); Bristol-Myers (2); Burroughs (3); Illinois Central Inds. (2); Studebaker-Worthington (2); Amer. Smelting & Refining (2); Eli Lilly (2); Corning Glass (3); Emerson Electric (2); Scott Paper (4); Carrier (3); Avco (2); Hewlett-Packard (2); Diamond Shamrock (RF&A); Cerro (2); Universal Oil Products (2); Int'l Minerals & Chemicals (RF&A); Cluett, Peabody (3); Carborundum (2); Sybron (4); Texas Gulf (2); Gannett (3); Ceco (2).

"Commercial Banking Companies: First National City Corp. (3); Chase Manhattan Corp. (David — RF&A+3); Manufacturers Hanover Corp. (5); Chemical New York Corp. (4); Bankers Trust New York Corp. (4); First Chicago Corp. (3); Marine Midland Banks, Inc. (3); Wells Fargo & Co. (2); Charter New York Corp. (2); Mellon National Corp. (3); First National Boston Corp. (3); National Detroit Corp. (5); Bank of New York Co. (2); Cleveland Trust Co. (2); Detroitbank Corp. (3); Lincoln First Banks, Inc. (RF&A); Southeast Banking Corp. (3).

"Life Insurance Companies: Prudential (5); Metropolitan (5); Equitable Life Assurance (3); New

York Life (2); Massachusetts Mutual (2); Mutual of New York (5); New England Mutual (2); Mutual Benefit (2).

"*Diversified Financial Companies:* American Express (6); Continental Corp. (4); CIT Financial (RF&A); Crum & Forster (RF&A).

"*Utilities:* American Telephone & Telegraph (5); Consolidated Edison (2); Detroit Edison (3).

"*Retailing Companies:* Great Atlantic & Pacific Tea (2); S.S. Kresge (RF&A + 1); Federated Department Stores (2); Winn-Dixie Stores (2); May Department Stores (2); R.H. Macy (RF&A + 4); Marriott (2).

"*Transportation Companies:* Pan American World Airways (4); Eastern Air Lines (RF&A + 3).

"*Companies Not Included in Fortune's Listing:* U.S. Trust Co. of New York (5); Fidelity Union Bankcorp, N.J. (4); J. Henry Schroder Banking Corp. (3); Bowery Savings Bank (3); Greenwich Savings Bank (RF&A + 1); Maccabees Mutual Life (2); Liberty Mutual Life (2); Reliance Insurance (2).

"*Canadian Corporations:* Investors Group (RF&S); Royal Bank of Canada (3); Investors Growth Fund (3); Investors Mutual of Canada (3); Great-Western Life Assurance (4); Montreal Trust Co. (2); Canadian Pacific Ltd. (2); International Nickel (2)."*

Notice that all the property listed in this report is valued at $640 billion. As great as is this amount, it is but a trifle

---

*The foregoing appraisal of the interlocking Rockefeller Empire was compiled six years ago, showed combined assets of all the companies listed at that time as being $640,000,000,000. That was before the Panama Canal deal that provided the international bankers another "sweetheart city."

compared to the wealth such men really own, mostly gained by and through their control of the nation's monetary system and the nation's government.

Their vaults hold many thousands of tons of gold.

To the above must be added the fact that these bankers are the chief holders of bonds and mortgages of $12 trillion of private and public debts and obligations, according to the National Taxpayers Union chart on page 116.

Then comes these bankers' ownership and leases of government property — land and sea, which they have gotten, in the main, for nothing. In this property there are countless trillions of dollars worth of natural resources — oil, natural gas, uranium, coal, shale and timber.

The foreign holdings of these men must not be forgotten. They hold claims for hundreds of billions of dollars of foreign debts, with interest, mostly uncollectable. (Firmly in control of our monetary system, they are requiring the United States taxpayers to pay.) Then there are their foreign branch banks, their foreign factories, their oil concessions, oil refineries, oil rigs. Almost all of these were acquired with wealth taken from the United States.

The Bottom Line

The wealth of our people has been sucked out. Their economy is an empty shell. There may be illusionary "recoveries" and "booms." If so, there is every reason to think that these will be followed by deeper plunges.

The Spoils of Unlimited Corporate Capitalism: Ownership of Property

Given now is the scale of proportionate ownership of all the vast wealth we have been discussing — the banks, the farmlands, the factories, the utilities, the minerals, oil, gas and coal.

It was compiled in 1975 — the last authentic calculations available to me. It is far greater now.

On this scale the financiers who control the United States government and its economy may be represented by the thickness of the top line. We include these as we move down the scale. One-tenth (1/10) of one (1) percent of our people own 62.8 percent of tax-exempt state and local bonds. About one (1) percent own 40 percent of the nation's wealth. One-sixth (1/6) own 82.4 percent of publicly held shares of the nation's corporations. Aside from their palaces, yachts, airplanes and works of art, most of the wealth of these upper divisions is productive wealth: banks, bonds, insurance companies, utilities, factories. The upper two percent of the nation's families own 33 times more investment property than is owned by the lower sixty percent.

The wealthier one percent of our population receives in yearly income more than eight times the total yearly income of all of the lower 50 percent of the population.

Concentration of Wealth
Vertical Line Represents People of the Nation

The Great Financiers are represented by thickness of top line. They control the nation.

1/10 of 1 percent own 62.8% of tax-exempt local government bonds.

The one percent of all adults (represented by the space between the two upper lines) own 40% of the wealth of the nation: money, banks, bonds, utilities, factories.

Families in the upper 2 percent own more than 33 times investment property than is owned by the lowest 60 percent.

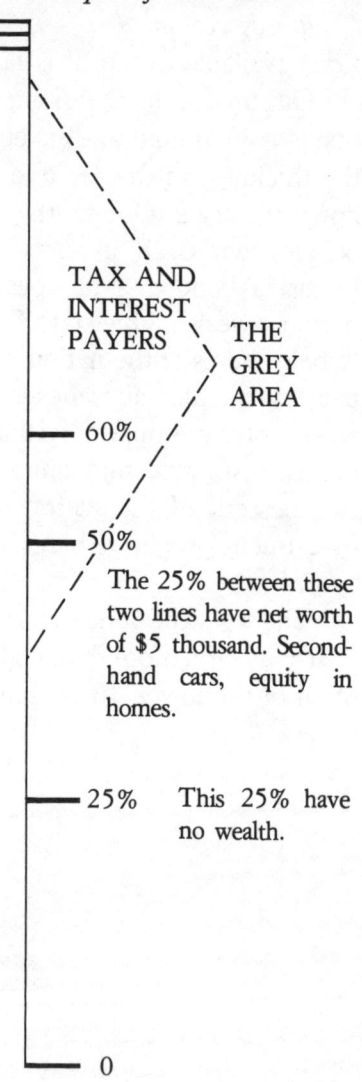

TAX AND INTEREST PAYERS

THE GREY AREA

— 60%

— 50%

The 25% between these two lines have net worth of $5 thousand. Second-hand cars, equity in homes.

— 25% This 25% have no wealth.

— 0

Scale: 1.3 millimeters = 1% of our people.

"Men who have created new fruit in the world cannot create a system whereby this fruit may be eaten."
John Steinbeck

CHAPTER 17

The Dregs of Exploitation

Our national debt ceiling has been increased six times in the last two and one-half years. It is now said to be $1.4 trillion. No estimate of its amount is accurate. In 1980 the budget deficit was said to be about $61 billion. The lead editorial of *The Asheville Citizen-Times,* October 12, 1980, stated that the highly respected accounting firm of W.M. O'Reilly & Company estimated the true deficit at $431 billion. Today's deficit is given at over $200 billion. It must be far more than that.

In addition to these debts there are here and abroad, all sorts of political debts and guarantees that are the taxpayers' liabilities. The *Congressional Record* of February 13, 1974, stated the Federal Housing Administration had insured $104 billion of residential mortgages. There have been nine years' addition to this.

Our total public debts, guarantees, and commitments and private debts are approximately twelve trillion dollars. Its interest must stagger the imagination.

Here is a report of a little transaction all of us can understand.

On March 4, 1974, the government borrowed 2.5 billion dollars for 91 days at 7.675 percent interest. This is a trifle as such things go, but when calculated we find that for this unnecessary favor the taxpayers must pay to the bankers $47,837,328.77 in interest.

Some idea of where the taxpayers' money goes in politically motivated projects may be gathered from the following:

Multibillion Synfuel earmarked $10 million for research grants. A letter from a researcher requesting a grant from this fund brought the following answer: "Sorry, only $1 million is left; the other $9 million has gone for administrative expenses."

The Small Business Administration has handed out many questionable loans.

According to Sidney Harris in *The Asheville Citizen* (2/20/79), out of the 34,000 or more companies that received Small Business Administration loans in the previous ten years, fewer than one percent were still in operation.

"Don't worry," we are told, "we owe the money to ourselves." The truth is, that we, the economic middle class, the real tax and interest payers, owe it to giant banks and corporations which are owned by a comparative handful of people.

The assertion that many millions of people own interest-bearing paper is misleading.

General public ownership of bonds and interest-bearing paper may be likened to public ownership of stock of which Frederick Lundsburg says in his book, *The Rich and the Super Rich:* "While twenty million or more stockholders have an equity (usually trifling) in these and hundreds of other companies, it is a fact, TNEC study showed, that from two to three up to twenty of the largest stockholders own very large total percentages of the companies. Small stockholders, are therefore, no more than insects crawling on the backs of a rhinoceros ... one who owns a share of stock worth 10 cents is classed as a stockholder."

Yet from Wall Street and financiers in general, the theme of wide ownership is constantly drummed in our ears with such words as the following: "The greater the number of individuals with a direct stake in our capitalistic system, the better the chances of surviving. It is very easy to talk about the flaws in our way of life in this country, to demean the free enterprise system, but once you have your money at stake you view things in a different light," according to G.G. McGreer in *Conquest of Poverty*.

They tell us that through his pension fund (holding stocks and bonds) the American laborer is a capitalist.

The following is evident:

(1) The laborer is not trusted to prepare for his own future.

(2) This is not true ownership. The laborer cannot pass these securities on to his descendants. He is only promised that if he does good and faithful work, remains with the company, and lives beyond retirement, he will be given enough of the dividend to support him for his remaining years.

(3) Many a laborer is in daily fear of losing his job and thus losing this promised security. Perhaps he is tired and would like to take a rest. However unhappy he may be with his work, however much he would like to quit and seek another job, he dares not. Such a man is not free.

(4) Most pensions are uncertain. At the very best full and honest payment of a pension is, and will be, available to a comparative few.

(5) And lastly, anyone who will take the pains to analyze the future of pensions must realize that the time will come when the system will bog down; that if pensions are

paid at all, they will be paid with almost worthless money.

In 1981 the *U.S. News & World Report* (5/25/81), reported that the Federal Employees' Pension Fund (supposedly surer than any of the others) was more than $400 billion in the red.

The following quotation is from G.G. McGreer, in *Conquest of Poverty:*

"Thus we have been led by the shallowest kind of trickery into the adoption and endurance of a system that has imposed poverty on the masses and persuaded them to accept the delusion that the people should remain mystified, perplexed, and poor, from fear that they will suffer disaster from plenty."

We have seen something of the lives of the creditors. Let us now look at the lives and prospects of the debtors.

"Poverty — the most deadly and prevalent of all diseases."
Eugene O'Neill

CHAPTER 18

The Dreary Life of Debt

Close to the upper lines of our economic scale come those who have good incomes, live in fine homes, and belong to the clubs. Some are in the professions. Most hold precarious jobs with large companies where high performance is demanded. Their lives are filled with strain. The prosperity of most of these is more illusionary than real. They save little. Taxes, debt with its interest, insurance, car expenses, and inflation see to that. A severe illness would be hard to manage. The loss of a job would bring a crisis in a month.

Below this stratum, wealth shades off rapidly into a gray area still above the middle line, representing millions of men and women who have little save a yearning for a better and more meaningful life for themselves and their children.

These are the people who directly or indirectly pay most of the taxes to support the government; pay interest on bonds; provide profits for the financiers and others who are in collusion with the government, and provide welfare checks for those still less fortunate.

Then there are property taxes on what little these people

do have; sales taxes, and taxes here and there on everything. Howard Jarvis determined that the $8,000 sticker price on his automobile included some $4,500 of taxes; that there are 116 taxes on a loaf of bread.

A man who has a job starting work on January 1st must work steadily far into May to pay his federal, state and local taxes. To this must be added his personal debts and their interest. He will work into August before making any money for himself.

The workers feel the strain. They know that something is wrong. They blame the people on welfare rather than the politicians and financiers who are really responsible.

The authorities do not deal as gently with such people as they do with great corporations that, through overcharges and tax evasion, conceal tens of billions of dollars. *The Asheville Citizen-Times* (11/12/72) stated that eight Charlotte welfare mothers of thirty-two dependent children had been jailed for not reporting that they had supplemented their welfare payments with pittances earned in menial jobs.

The Miami Herald for January 18, 1974, reported that the Internal Revenue Service was conducting a special investigation of housewives who work four or five hours a day attending the sick in their homes.

Men in this gray area, together with their wives, work long and well, and moonlight, and still fall behind. Their children are often adrift and bewildered.

Conditions have worsened. *The U.S. News and World Report* (3/19/84) states that 57.2% of mothers with children under 18 work outside the home, and more than half of all children have working mothers. Various proposals are advanced as how to best care for these children. There is no mention of the true solution: an economic system that would allow the mothers to stay at home.

The Self-Employed

Here and there is a man with enough enterprise to start a business for himself. Very little can be done unless he is first financed — that is, without borrowing at interest. He runs into a maze of regulations — the trying demands of bureaucrats. Our new businessman has borrowed a fixed amount that must be returned. There is never an overage for interest. All borrowers are attempting to get money to pay interest. The chances that all can meet this ever-increasing infinite charge is simply non-existent.

And all the while the government is calling for taxes on the new venture. Its owner is required to fill out, under dire threats, endless agonizing forms. He is required to report, under penalty, every three months, his income and pay its tax.

Every dollar he gets is put on computers and followed. Bank debts, due to interest charges, multiply. Few of these small enterprises succeed.

On an ABC newscast, April 7, 1982, it was stated that in the year before 30,000 small businesses had declared bankruptcy, and probably as many as 500,000 more had quietly closed.

Home

A man and his wife want a home. They have been able to save very little; taxes, payroll deductions and hidden expenses have seen to that. They borrow the money — in reality nothing but a permit to allow them to build on credit. They take upon themselves long years of debt and strain. Closing charges and insurance are high. The cost of land, material and construction are high; yet, in the long view these are not the main cost.

Interest — the charge for use of money that financiers create for nothing but clerical charges — is the main cost. This interest may run up the total cost of the house — in long-term cases, to three or four times the purchase price: architect's fee, the price of lumber, the brick, heating plant, wiring and labor. Yes, even after these have absorbed all hidden taxes and the interest paid by contractors on construction loans, there will be the huge interest on the mortgage itself.

For, as it happens, a clear example, I include the following: Recently an acquaintance made a $44,000 down payment on a house. On September 9, 1983, he obtained a $100,000 loan for the balance. His mortgage payments will be $1,000 a month for 30 years — a total of $360,000.

Had the interest been three percent higher, as many pay, the total would be $450,000.

Early in April, 1980, President Carter signed into Federal law a bill which struck down all state laws that put a limit on the amount of interest that may be charged on building loans. The President praised this terrible law as a great help to those who need a home. Since then the average monthly payments to buy a home have doubled.

An ABC newscast, June 14, 1982, stated that the average house now costs $74,000, and that monthly payments, insurance, and taxes are $483 each month.

There is never an easy day or night for a person forced to meet such payments for so many years. The specter of the loss of a job, of illness, of death — to say nothing of just weariness — makes his life a nightmare. And then there is the upkeep of the home, needed appliances and furniture, and cars and their care (needed to go to work).

Few people can buy a home now, but that does not bother the bankers, nor induce them to lower interest rates. Firmly in control of Congress, bankers have got the United

States government into an extension of the money market. The government has become the bankers' middle man. It pays any interest requested. It gives absolute security on every loan, no matter how questionable, and furnishes great "now" profits.

Down the Scale

Look again at the diagram on page 168.

Twenty-five percent of our citizens (below the middle line) have a net worth of no more than $5,000. This is not productive wealth. It consists of a few personal belongings, an old car, an equity in furniture and in a mortgaged home. Most of the wealth they seem to have is illusionary.

The 1983 *World Almanac,* under automobiles, installment credit, for 1982, gives the amount drivers owed on their automobiles as $128,415,000,000.

These citizens, too, like those in the gray area above, are being stripped of their earnings to pay inordinate profits and taxes; to support an army of welfare workers, and to divide with the impoverished. Struggling under this burden and that of soaring inflation, these men and women also, one by one, and by the thousands, sink further down the scale.

The following letter speaks for millions of Americans. It was clipped from ACTION LINE, *The Miami Herald,* March 10, 1977:

> "For the last few years I've been under constant pressure from bills and mortgage payments. Everything is getting worse instead of better. I'm working three jobs to keep things going. I can't take it any more. Please tell me what to do. Mrs. _____"

Under the heading, "Golden Years — A Bitter Joke for Most," Bob Dennis, in the *Charlotte Observer* (6/22/69), says: "Instead of allowing its citizens to keep most of their earnings, the government has, through their productive years, taken from them as Social Security and taxes, their hard-earned, valuable dollars, and now in their old age pauperized them by allowing inflation to cheapen their refund to a pittance — leaving them helpless in the hands of the sociologist."

The aged are not the only victims of an economic system totally slanted to profits for the rich. Many able-bodied, hard working men with young families have been forced out of line. Once most of these citizens had the security of a few acres of land and a garden, but not any more. Once they could start a little business or service, but great corporations have pre-empted most of these. These citizens have been herded in for a dull, precarious life in the slums of a city.

The Hopeless

Below these are another twenty-five percent (a full fifty million of our people) who have nothing of value unless it be the clothes on their backs and perhaps a small amount of money in their pockets.

For some large cities whole sections, 90% of the inhabitants, are on welfare.

As far back as 1968, state, local and federal spending was $112.4 billion. In New York City one person in eight is on welfare. To disguise the name "welfare," the department has been renamed "The Department of Health and Human Service." It has some 140,000 employees. Its budget is some $300 billion a year. Soon half of all taxes collected will be dispersed by this agency. Over 22,200,000 of our citizens are receiving food stamps. The number is to be cut somewhat in fiscal 1985, provided politicians can bring themselves to do that.

Our officials are careful that taxes for this do not fall upon the wealthy.

Planners, saddled upon us by the politicians, their pay extracted from the taxpayers, are forever attempting to set things right by calling on the federal government for funds (to be obtained by raising taxes or selling bonds), and then calling on local authorities for matching funds, to put some little scheme into effect. If on a vote the citizens defeat the bond issue, the planners at once try again. They change the wording of the act so that if you want to vote against it you must vote "yes." Now going into the slums to get out those voters who pay little or no taxes, and treading softly in the rest of the city, they hold the election. Individual homeowners are helpless.

Government projects condemn whole sections of small homes and businesses, some highly prized by their owners, and taken for a trifle and bulldozed down. The displaced owners become renters in government-owned apartments, crowded in with uncongenial neighbors.

For these people life loses much of its meaning. The deepest instinct in a human being is the desire to own its own home, a little patch of land, a tree.

The government's program to provide homes has met with little success. Interest rates and political corruption have played their part. Shoddy workmanship and maintenance and increasing poverty, along with the very nature of such a program, have turned clusters of these buildings into miserable slums. As far back as October 24, 1974, Paul Harvey stated that the government was owner of 78,000 abandoned homes. In Atlanta, April 1981, volunteers searching for clues of slain black children prowled through a federally-subsidized apartment complex. About 860 of the 1,100 apartments were vacant, their doors battered down, their windows broken — a haven for criminals.

Broken windows are not the only consequences of such an existence. There are broken bodies. On May 6, 1980, Paul Harvey said that the doctors at Johns Hopkins believe, more and more, that high blood pressure and heart disease are prone to follow stress.

Broken Lives

The Battered Child Syndrome is no new thing. Lately it has increased alarmingly. Such violence has spread to the family. Under the heading, "Battered Families: A Growing Nightmare," *U.S. News & World Report* (1/15/79) states: "At the root of many of these incidences are money and job worries, and inability to cope with an increasingly complicated world."

And on May 6, 1980, *The Miami Herald* devoted a large spread to family violence: "Home Is Where the Heartbreak Is." The paper states that in half the homes of the nation violence is a constant factor. Husbands beat wives; a baby crying at night or a child wetting the bed may be killed. Children fight each other; sons and daughters beat their aged parents. The paper listed eight nearby shelters for these beaten people. Teenagers are not the only ones who run away, or are driven from home. Each year some 25,000 of the aged, who are unwanted, "who can't take it any longer" run away and out into the world to perish.

Many millions of our people own no home. A half million are classed as "homeless." Dressed in tatters, scavenging for food and often suffering from severe emotional problems, there are tens of thousands of such people in most large cities. Many must sleep on park benches or on the gratings of sidewalks. In bitter cold weather the authorities send trucks around each morning to pick up those who have frozen to death in the night.

In spite of all this it was reported, *U.S. News & World Report* (11/28/83), that the government is bringing in 72,000 paupers, paying their way, and will provide for them after their arrival.

President Reagan states that the federal government cannot afford to provide for all our indigent citizens, and appeals to churches and local citizens to help. Not once have I heard him appeal to the fabulously wealthy bankers for aid. He wants to give them a handout. For them it is billions of dollars to pay defaulted foreign loans with interest.

The Dole

Instead of improving the economic climate for small, free enterprise, making it possible for people to support themselves, the federal government, raising taxes and the government debt, increased the dole.

This has gone from bad to worse. At every election the politicians promise more. There are food stamps, housing, and all sorts of aids and unsecured loans. Raising taxes and increasing the government debt, the government passed a law extending aid to fatherless families. This is based on the number of children. Many men, unemployed, or making little, left their families in order that they might qualify for this money.

As of 1980 forty-two percent of black families were headed by a female — often with many children. The *U.S. News & World Report* (5/10/82), stated that in the District of Columbia: "580 per 1,000 live births are illegitimate."

For all that these women have more children than many married ones. A woman who gets up before dawn, gets breakfast and then goes out and works all day to help her husband pay for a place to live and buy the necessary cars, has neither the money, the time nor the strength to have children and care for them. Married couples in this nation average less than two children; *Reader's Digest* (4/84) says 1.8 children.

Once on the dole the tendency is to adjust one's life to government poverty requirements in order to get the largest possible handouts. Government support has moved millions of people into the leisure class. Even in the depression, and even at high wages it is difficult to hire anyone for common labor. On April 9, 1982, I called Nettlewood Nursery, at Asheville, N.C. "No," was the answer. "We can sell you the plants and tell you how to plant them, but we can't put them in for you. We can't hire any help."

It is difficult to get anyone to cut the grass, to get help to clean the kitchen. Natives will not pick strawberries or beans. They will not cut sugarcane.

Millions of people have no conception of the relationship of honest labor and its reward.

Receiving some six or eight thousand dollars a year for doing nothing, a man has no incentive to work for that much, to say nothing of the great tax deductions from his take home pay. If in addition to welfare the man has been getting food stamps, medicine and a rent subsidy, his calculated tax deductions may run as high as sixty or seventy percent.

This seemingly adequate income from job, or dole, has little purchasing power. The goods purchased are designed for profit rather than for quality and good measure. A high priced bag of groceries from the supermarket contains a wastebasket of printed wrappers, cardboard boxes, aluminum foil, cellophane, cans, and little food.

There are some 46 million people on welfare of one kind or another, and many more assisted by local charities. There are all sorts of other government help for the poor. This year of 1984, there will be 100,000 additional subsidized houses, 40,000 apartments. There will be help in paying fuel bills.

CHAPTER 19

Federal Intrusion

It seems that every government intrusion into local affairs has worsened them.

We once had good public schools — in the North where there was peaceful integration, and in the South where we should have had it. Instead of enforcing this one point, and allowing local authorities to continue to operate their schools, the federal government came in. Insisting on giving federal aid to public schools, it created a large bureau to control them. There were bussing, rules for hiring, protecting and promoting incompetent teachers. Textbooks were changed and in many places inane, filthy books were forced in use, against the protest of parents. Basic subjects gave way to social studies, with sex education.

One of my early schools was a one-room log building. It had all grades and one teacher — Miss Rosa Hemphill. She was devoted to the children, and they to her. There was earnestness there and high purpose. I sometimes think of that school when I pass a fine present-day school building with its champion basketball team. Its children are beaten and robbed on the playgrounds. Teachers are raped.

Teachers are stabbed to death in their classrooms. Many graduates cannot read and understand a written page.

Through the forced lowering of university standards for admission to accommodate these unprepared graduates; by the forced employment of incompetent teachers; by the imposition of a flood of paperwork and senseless regulations, the government has also seriously injured our once-great system of higher education. The effect is far-reaching. It is felt everywhere — not only here, but in our standing throughout the world.

Instead of conducting the affairs of this country in such a way that there would be little poverty, and letting local authorities care for the indigent, the federal government, raising taxes, passed a law extending government aid to fatherless families. In order to qualify for this welfare, many men left their families. A fine black man told me that in his section many girls had baby after baby by any man that came along in order to qualify for this money. He was distressed. He said it was ruining his race. In the District of Columbia, 580 per 1,000 live births are illegitimate.

As of 1980 forty-two percent of black families were headed by a female, often with many children. Many men, some without jobs, others having large taxes taken from their wages, are freed from the responsibility of caring for their families. Along with jobless teenagers they roam the streets. Many take to drink, to drugs and some take to crime.

The third generation is now on welfare. Unemployment among black teenagers is 53 percent. To these millions are added millions more every year. They will vote and demand a larger handout.

For those people who work and pay taxes for all this, it is a different story. It costs money to raise children and most people don't have it. Women who work all day cannot bear children and care for them. The average family in the United States has less than two children (1.8).

Affirmative Action

White males, who should be at work allowing their wives to stay at home to care for the children, are denied work. Often the jobs are given to minorities or to women.

Government contracts are given to minorities without bidding. On one such contract that comes to mind the black did not undertake the work. This job was then opened for bids. The winning bid was a little more than half as much as the former contract.

On an ABC newscast, December 9, 1983, it was reported that in one western city where there was easy and friendly integration, there were on one side of the city 50 small government houses for retired people. All of these were occupied by white people. On the other side of the city a government housing project had 50 mostly larger units for larger families. These were occupied by blacks. A federal judge ordered that this be changed, that 25 families of whites be moved into the black settlement, and that 25 blacks be shifted to the vacated houses. All this though none of the families wanted to leave their neighbors and friends.

This speaks of coercion in a nation which is no longer altogether free.

The Bill Collector

Our national debt has seemed as unreal as some pagan deity for whom we have been required to sacrifice and pay tribute. Now, all at once, this debt becomes a stark reality. The financiers who hold the bonds are pressing for payment — not of interest but of principal. The demand is that the government sell its property and pay. None of the rest of us have any money to buy. The financiers intend to credit the property's appraised price as partial payment on the debt and take the property over.

Since this takeover was first proposed it has been put in different words. It is said to start with the budget deficit. As this is, in reality, but a current debt to the financiers, it amounts to the same thing. (Two bills providing for this have been introduced: one, H.R. 265, by Rep. Larry Winn [R-KS], and S.R. 231 by Senator Charles Percy [R-IL])

On an NBC newscast, February 25, 1982, there were shown a number of fine pieces of government property being considered for sale. There were buildings, military campsites and beach-front property in Hawaii. Then came the real object of the movement: a map of the United States showing shaded government land. There were splashes here and there and a wide shadow passing down through the Rocky Mountain States from Canada to Mexico — in all, over 564,000 square miles of government-owned land that holds timber, oil, gas, coal, shale, uranium and other materials. In that strip there are almost unlimited resources and almost unbelievable wealth. And then there is Alaska's 340,000 square miles to give bond holders.

All this is but a start — a foot in the door. The debt, created by manipulations in computers, continuing, rolling up like a giant snowball will, at the end, take all property — both public and private.

There is much more danger in this situation than is generally realized. In accordance with the *Constitution,* Section 8, Paragraph 1, Congress must pay government debts, presumably by taxation, when due and on demand. The President, always put into office by the bankers, is charged by the *Constitution* with enforcing the law — in this case payment of the nation's debts. It makes no difference how the debts were incurred.

Under Emergency Executive Order number 12148, placed into law July 20, 1979, the President may, on his order alone, declare a state of emergency and take dictatorial power. He may freeze bank accounts above a small stated amount, commandeer all food, commandeer all property, shift people about, put them to work at any job — and, of course, enforce taxation to pay the public debt.

When this executive order was placed into law there was little fear of war. If there had been, there was no need to provide for limiting the amount of money a person could withdraw from his bank. There was no such restriction in former wars.

CHAPTER 20

A Glance Backward and a Look Ahead

Here, to check the spelling of a name I had used, I went to a large box of carefully packed clippings. At a glance I recognized each clipping and laid it aside. Sometimes I would see one I had used. Finally I grew weary and hopeless. The next day I was at it again. I pulled out great slabs of clippings — all I could hold in my two hands. One by one I examined and restacked them.

In that mass of material is the solid evidence upon which this book is built. It could only touch the material here and there.

As I worked I became aware of a startling fact. Almost all of the clippings dealt with the actions of a comparative handful of men.

I looked out of the window and saw the green forest, and thought of the marvelous world that God has given us, of the wonderful nation our forefathers built, of its many inhabitants of kind, earnest, industrious, honest people — now caught in the vise.

I then looked back, in sorrow, at what I had been impelled to write, but it is true. These things, all these things, have become a part of our lives.

Columnist Walter Williams has said that our government is more oppressive than was the government of George III.

Government reports and most economists have stated that the recent depression ended in December 1982. Now, a year later, the stock market is booming. Great banks are building their skyscrapers. The news tells of the nation's awakening — of its great economic gains.

"When will it reach us?" is the question being asked by the millions of the unemployed, the hundreds of thousands who have lost their homes, and those tens of thousands who are in arrears with their monthly payments, the tens of millions who have never had anything to lose.

Unless there is a real reform, except for a token improvement, the answer is never.

Kitty Goodman, director of the Community Food Resources Center in New York, says: "We have seen things become worse, and worse and worse. The economy is not getting better in poor neighborhoods." Rita Rosenberg, another director, said, "The plea for help has risen 116 percent in the past year."

The same story is heard across the nation. Ruth Sterling, director of North West Second Harvest in Seattle, said: "Food distribution in the first six months of 1983 more than doubled over the same period a year earlier and four times the 1981 level."

Considering all these things, it is clear that the inner health and well-being of our nation cannot be expressed in terms of national wealth; that is, by recounting the great wealth of a few financiers.

The real story is told by a look at the fiscal condition, safety and honor of our government and the prosperity and happiness of our average citizen.

The zest has gone from American life. Depression is widespread. "According to the National Mental Health Association, approximately 30 million Americans — one in seven — suffer some form of mental or emotional disease."

To hope that inequality will level out, that taxes will be lowered, that the stress and strain of life will lessen, is but to indulge in a wistful dream.

Behind the flurry in the stock market and all the drum beating lies the dismal truth. For most people the depression is not over, and unless there is a drastic change, never will be. All the optimism and promises from politicians and financiers simply means that they are looking to the next election, and hope that these will keep them in their positions of privilege and power.

It is for us — the people who love our nation, to set things right. And we can.

The solution is a return to the *Constitution*.

THE SOLUTION

CHAPTER 21

Regaining Our Government: A Return to the *U.S. Constitution*

The foundation of America was solidly built upon the footings of the Bible and three great documents: *The Mayflower Compact, The Declaration of Independence,* and *The Constitution of the United States of America.*

The solution to all of our national problems will be found in a return to these. Since they should be in every home, they are included in the Appendix of this book. The following, easily understood suggestions are based on them and, in addition, offer hope for completeness and permanency.

Reform must start with the grassroots, dry as tinder from long abuse by financiers and politicians. Evidences of the early brush fires of sweeping change can already be seen on the horizon. There are thousands of patriotic organizations which have sprung up in recent years, many of them spreading the word through publications.

Scattered throughout our nation are millions of people who know we must return to the wording and intent of the original *Constitution* and provide safeguards for it. Some of these write letters to the editor for their local papers; others call into talk shows to express their views; still others photocopy or buy in quantity important information to alert their families and friends.

These patriots could succeed if one of them in each Congressional district would ferret out the others, encourage them to study the foundational documents, and come together to talk of these things. Copies of both *Honest Money* and *Honest Government* could be read by the members of such groups over a period of months. Each should go among his neighbors and friends with the word.

The Independent Voters' Party

Such activists should form the Independent Voters' Party; that is, they should, as a group, vote for Constitutional candidates of any party. The Founding Fathers of our country never spoke of a two-party system. It was invented by the financiers who named the Presidential candidates of both parties. Then they have left it for the voters to decide between the two evils.

The state of the union revealed in this book cannot be convincingly told in brief political campaigns. It must be read. It must be told in letters to newspapers; articles in the free press; in meetings in homes, halls, highways and byways; year in and year out.

Once, patriotism and the determination to throw off oppressive rule swept through this country with great fervor. The Sons of Liberty who signed *The Declaration of Independence* pledged their lives, their fortunes, their sacred honor — for freedom. Many had to deliver on that pledge. Can we do less and hope to succeed?

Elections

We have seen our nation decline from its position of integrity, prosperity, world influence, and power because of corruption. Candidates obligate themselves to donors of campaign expenses who have high financial stakes in their future actions.

We can put an end to this.

Representatives

The first office to free in election reform is that of U.S. representative — the local one — filled every two years. If the incumbent, be he Republican or Democrat, is acceptable in moral character and intelligent, he should be approached and asked to read this book. If he is willing to swear, in public, that he will use his office in a continuous attempt to restore such constitutional reforms, the group should vote for him in a body.

If he will not agree to this commitment, the group should offer their support, under the same terms, to any candidate of either political party who will. Failing here, they should nominate a candidate from their own group, preferably in time to file in one of the two major party primaries. This playing in and out of the major parties will soon have its effect.

During the transition process back to constitutional government, we must work within the parameters of present traditions. When the Congress is firmly established under constitutional authority, by genuine patriots, the rules should be changed to conform to the intent of the Founding Fathers.

Eventually, anyone offering himself as a candidate for U.S. representative should be required to present petitions of signatures of registered voters approving his candidacy to the election board. (Independent candidates are required to do that today, in many states.)

During the campaign the Congressional district (or area

covered by whatever office is at stake) should be an island. No one outside its borders should be allowed to aid or interfere in any way. Those in the Congressional district who are willing should volunteer their services. There should be *no* paid, political advertising with any media outlet. Newspapers, local radio and television stations which hold free franchises to free use of the airwaves, should be required to give equal time to all qualified candidates. They should not be permitted to add their own comments to those of the candidates. (Their editorial comments come under their guarantee of free speech.) Places and times of political meetings, as well as brief summaries of each candidate's views, should be accorded, along with candidates' statements of their qualifications, philosophies, and purposes.

Contributions

Both contributions and the spending of money in behalf of any candidate should be forbidden by federal law. This includes the gift of money or valuable favor to any candidate or official, or their families, by anyone who may have a personal interest in his official actions. The penalty for this should be disqualification, and long prison terms for both giver and taker of the bribe.

Polls

Published polls during elections may influence the outcome. Such polls are subject to misuse.

Free speech is one thing. The unmonitored and uncontrolled publication of what others think and say in these important cases is quite another.

Polls in elections should be forbidden.

Senators

The 17th Amendment, allowing candidates to be elected to the U.S. Senate by popular vote, should be repealed. Then state legislators would again select Senate candidates from the state's finest men and women. This selection would be without cost, and U.S. senators could again take office without any obligation except that of serving all the nation's people, to the best of their ability.

The Presidency

The method now used for electing the President and Vice President is clearly unconstitutional. Nowhere does that great document say that a Presidential candidate shall be chosen in a national convention of a political party. Nowhere does it give a Presidential candidate the power to choose his running mate.

The College of Electors was not meant to be a rubber stamp. That College was charged with the duty of choosing the nation's greatest men for America's highest offices. The President, so chosen, was not under obligation to anyone.

Congress and Courts for Reform

Congress now has power to order the return to the *Constitution*, and this should be insisted upon.

It would be well if some patriotic group should bring suit in the Superior Court to stop political parties from choosing the President and Vice President, and for the return of this privilege and duty to the Electoral College.

The Supreme Court

To free the Supreme Court from all outside influences and obligations, and to insure a rule of law and not of men, it would be well to amend the *Constitution* as to its choice. These justices should be chosen from among the nation's finest lawyers: from among the Chief Justices of the states' Supreme Courts.

Even then, Congress, as now provided by the *Constitution*, should have the final word.

How much better this would be than to allow the Court, year after year, to persist in a course that tears the whole nation apart.

Needed Constitutional Reforms

The Balanced Budget-Tax Limitation Amendment has already been approved by 32 state legislatures. Once two more states pass this amendment, Congress must act — either to pass the amendment and make it part of our *Constitution,* or to call a constitutional convention for this purpose. Most patriots prefer the former option, since a "Con-Con" has the potential of opening the proverbial can of worms. If radical elements seized control of such a convention, they would try to do away with the *Constitution* itself, destroying the sovereignty of the United States. This has long been the goal of One-World globalists. The same congressmen who signed the infamous "Declaration of *Inter*dependence" in Philadelphia in 1976 could be expected to overthrow the *Constitution* if they were given the opportunity. This must not be allowed to happen.

For information about the Balanced Budget-Tax Limitation Amendment in your state and for excellent information on the total picture, write: National Taxpayers' Union, 315

Pennsylvania Avenue, S.E., Washington, D.C. 20003.

Letters and visits to congressmen should stress the need of these three amending reforms for our *Constitution*.

The Sixteenth Amendment

The 16th Amendment, creating the graduated, personal income tax, should be repealed. Many groups across the nation are working toward this end. The amendment was passed in 1913, just as the Federal Reserve Act was. Astute economists have long recognized that the real purpose for this Trojan Horse was to provide the interest inherent in the Federal Reserve System with its endemic deficit spending.

The Right Road

There is another way, a higher, nobler philosophy than any we have tried. This nation should proclaim it. It is:

Fair Play and Simple Honesty

Efficiency, stability, safety, honesty and personal liberty are all attributes of a true republic. To these should be added firmness for the right.

Our forefathers gave us the *Constitution,* the best government ever devised. It is for us to purge the nation of its evils and take up where they left off.

When, finally, true reformers emerge or are elected, they will find their corrective efforts restrained by hundreds of laws and regulations — enacted to confer special favors on former contributors — many more than a century old. Every such act should be sought out and repealed.

The importance of pushing now for these reforms is incalculable. Communism and world federalism promise alike, however falsely, an Eden for the hopeless. As poverty and despair spread, dictatorial government follows. It has engulfed nation after nation. The waves are lapping at our own shores.

Prompt reforms of the following problems and injustices are essential.

Labor Unions

Once monopolies are controlled, labor unions can rightfully be denied a free hand, and put in their proper place as helpful parts of the whole.

Industrialists have named the incessant demands of labor unions, backed by violence and threats, as reasons for carrying their factories overseas. This reaction by the industrialists creates millions of the unemployed, and opens the way to a flood of foreign goods, creating more unemployment. When this is stopped, and American factories once again operate in America with American labor, the factories must be protected from arbitrary action by unions.

Compound unions should be broken into their component parts, and collusion between these parts forbidden. Membership in any one union should be limited to workers in one particular field.

The government should form a neutral board with power to arbitrate contentions between labor and employers in vital public works. In all other conducted businesses, in farms, and in households, an agreement to work or not to work, and the amount of wage, should be a matter of agreement between employers and employees.

Of course laborers should be free to strike — that is, to stop work — if they want to do so. They should not be allowed to picket the struck plant, or in any way interfere with the hiring of replacements. No worker who gives up his job should be given unemployment or other benefits from the government — that is, from those who work.

Labor unions should not be allowed to limit the number of craftsmen. There is a dearth of carpenters, plumbers and electricians. The right to learn a trade and to work at it without harrassment and danger from anyone is inherent in the *Constitution's* guarantee of life, liberty and the pursuit of happiness.

People need homes, and they need cheaper ones.

Monopolies

This is a new day!

The cliché "Free Enterprise" can no longer be accepted as justification for the freedom of a group of powerful financiers to lay claim to whatever they want, to choke all competition, and, gaining monopoly on a necessity of life, raise its price in order to pile up vast fortunes — to repeat the process in other fields.

Great monopolistic combines, conglomerates, cartels, and international corporations operating here must be broken up into smaller, honestly competing companies, the field of these sharply limited. Each corporation should operate in its own related field only.

The "Free Trade Treaty" that President Carter signed should be revoked. Products and parts made in our citizens' foreign factories should be denied entry to the United States.

No chartered company operating in other fields should be allowed to own agriculture land. Those owning it now should be given a reasonable time to dispose of it to unrelated individuals. There should be no government subsidies. As there is no end to the greed of some men it would be well to limit the amount of farm produce any one man is allowed to raise and sell.

The underlying purpose of all charters granted should be true private enterprise, and the prevention of monopoly on the necessities of life.

Corporate Taxes

In accordance with ideas expressed earlier, it is felt that every tax on corporations, producing goods for sale, along with every other hidden tax should be repealed. The people should know, plainly and exactly, how much taxes they pay. Any needed federal excise tax should be placed as a sales tax, in retail stores. Such a tax — highest on luxuries — would be just, and easy to collect.

Bureaucratic Interference

The safety of the nation and its health comes first. After that there need be little interference by bureaucrats. Some workers are more skilled, more dedicated, more productive than others. There should be no effort by the government to force equality. This lowers the national standard. The government laws as to hiring practices, and wages, should be repealed. Returning factories must be freed from most government paper work.

Monetary Reform

Monetary reform is vital. Without it all other reforms are meaningless.

Suggestions for this reform are in my former book, *Honest Money*. Congress should repeal the Federal Reserve Act of 1913. It should then issue and control the United States Note as our only money. This could be done very simply by increasing the amount of United States Notes which, though rare, are still in circulation and still legal tender. In the hundred and twenty years since Lincoln first issued these notes, they have cost nothing but the printing. Under the proposed new system, most interest from loans would come to the government to help with taxes.

Our officials should then acknowledge the nation's honest debts and as soon as possible pay them. Most of our debts were not created by service to the nation. They were created by trickery, bribery of public officials, and then by manipulations of figures on paper or in a computer. There are trillions of dollars of such debts. All the people working for a thousand years could not pay them in any way except to surrender all property. Debts created by manipulations on paper should be paid by manipulations on paper.

Gifts and Inheritances

Inflationary appraisals and the high taxes of today rule out many sizable gifts. Often the settlement of an estate is a sordid affair, with lawyers and tax collectors contending for as large a share as possible.

A man who has spent his life at honest labor, and has paid his taxes, should have full ownership of his earnings. They belong to him; not the government. He should be allowed to freely give his estate to whom he chooses.

There should be no tax credit for any gift. Such allowances invite sharp practices and are wrong in principle. When no one is allowed to avoid just taxes, the climate will also be right to deny any right to say how those taxes are used. (Our full say will be at the polls for honest candidates, and keeping in touch with them later so that they reflect their views in responsible legislation.)

Natural Resources

Natural resources in government land and waters should be a source of revenue for all our people.

It is suggested that leases of areas rich in natural resources be contracted, allowing the operating companies cost plus a fair percentage of profits for handling, and that the bulk of the profits be taken by the Treasury and used to reduce taxes.

Those tracts already leased, obtained through election of federal officials obligated to great companies, should be rewritten to conform to the above.

National Sovereignty

The oath of allegiance is all but forgotten.

When our people regain their government, one of their first concerns should be to sharply draw our boundary lines and reassert our nationality — the United States of America. We should resign from the United Nations, and force that organization out of our country.

Peacetime attempts by internationalists to destroy our national sovereignty are as dangerous as such actions in war. Such subversions should be made a felony.

We should examine every action which the internationalists have forced upon us, and rescind every one which harms this nation.

A Final Word

If everyone who reads this will talk about it with his neighbors, and with these form small political units, and bringing these together, form an Independent Voters Party, this party can choose and elect its own officials — sworn publically, to enact these reforms.

Last May, the long dreary winter had passed. After writing the last paragraph I chanced to look out of the window. The forest, the whole view was filled with fresh green leaves. It was breathtaking. It seemed impossible that all this had happened, as if in a single night. I then realized that it had been accomplished because each twig had done its bit.

We can have an honest government, and soon, if each of us will lend a hand, and seek the One whose power will make it possible.

"If my people, which are called by my name, shall humble themselves, and pray, and seek my face, and turn from their wicked ways; then will I hear from heaven, and will forgive their sin, and will heal their land" (II Chronicles 7:14).

APPENDIX

The Three Greatest Documents of American History in Chronological Order

The Mayflower Compact (1620)

The Declaration of Independence (1776)

The Constitution of the United States of America (1789)

APPENDIX A

The Mayflower Compact, 1620

"In the Name of God, Amen. We, whose names are underwritten, the Loyal Subjects of our dread Sovereign Lord King James, by the Grace of God, of Great Britain, France, and Ireland, King, Defender of the Faith, etc. Having undertaken for the Glory of God, and Advancement of the Christian Faith, and the Honour of our King and Country, a Voyage to plant the first Colony in the northern parts of Virginia; Do by these Presents, solemnly and mutually, in the Presence of God and one another, covenant and combine ourselves together into a civil Body Politick, for our better Ordering and Preservation, and Furtherance of the Ends aforesaid: And by Virtue hereof do enact, constitute, and frame, such just and equal Laws, Ordinances, Acts, Constitutions, and Officers, from time to time, as shall be thought most meet and convenient for the general Good of the Colony; unto which we promise all due Submission and Obedience. In Witness whereof we have hereunto subscribed our names at Cape-Cod the eleventh of November, in the Reign of our Sovereign Lord King James, of England, France, and Ireland, the eighteenth, and of Scotland, the fifty-fourth, Anno Domini 1620."

APPENDIX B

The Declaration of Independence

In Congress July 4, 1776

The Unanimous Declaration of the Thirteen United States of America

When in the course of human events, it becomes necessary for one people to dissolve the political bands which have connected them with another, and to assume among the powers of the earth, the separate and equal station to which the Laws of Nature and of *Nature's God* entitles them, a decent respect to the opinions of mankind requires that they should declare the causes which impel them to the separation.

We hold these truths to be self-evident, that all men are created equal, that they are endowed by their *Creator* with certain unalienable Rights, that among these are Life, Liberty and the pursuit of Happiness. That to secure these rights, Governments are instituted among Men, deriving their just powers from the consent of the governed. That whenever any Form of Government becomes destructive of these ends, it is the Right of the People to alter or to abolish it, and to institute new Government, laying its foundation on such principles and organizing its powers in such form, as to them shall seem most likely to effect their Safety and Happiness. *Prudence,* indeed, will dictate that Governments long established should not be changed for light and transient causes; and accordingly all experience hath shewn, that mankind are more disposed to suffer, while evils are sufferable, than to right themselves by abolishing the forms to which they are accustomed. But when a long train of abuses and usurpations, pursuing invariably the same Object, evinces a design to reduce them under absolute Despotism, it is their right, it is their duty, to throw off such Government, and to provide new Guards for their future security. Such has been the patient sufferance of these Colonies; and such is now the necessity which constrains them to alter their former Systems of Government. The history of the present King of Great Britain is a history of repeated injuries and usurpations, all having in direct object the establishment of an absolute Tyranny over these States. To prove this, let Facts be submitted to a candid world.

He has refused his Assent to Laws, the most wholesome and necessary for the public good.

He has forbidden his Governors to pass Laws of immediate and pressing importance, unless suspended in their operation till his Assent should be obtained; and when so suspended, he has utterly neglected to attend to them.

He has refused to pass other Laws for the accommodation of large districts of people, unless those people would relinquish the right of Representation in the Legislature, a right inestimable to them and formidable to tyrants only.

He has called together legislative bodies at places unusual, uncomfortable, and distant from the depository of their public Records, for the sole purpose of fatiguing them into compliance with his measures.

He has dissolved Representative Houses repeatedly, for opposing with manly firmness his invasions on the rights of the people.

He has refused for a long time, after such dissolutions, to

cause others to be elected; whereby the Legislative powers, incapable of Annihilation, have returned to the People at large for their exercise; the State remaining in the meantime exposed to all the dangers of invasion from without, and convulsions within.

He has endeavored to prevent the population of these States; for that purpose obstructing the Laws for Naturalization of Foreigners; refusing to pass others to encourage their migrations hither, and raising the conditions of new Appropriations of Lands.

He has obstructed the Administration of Justice, by refusing his Assent to Laws for establishing Judiciary Powers.

He has made Judges dependent on his Will alone, for the tenure of their offices, and the amount and payment of their salaries.

He has erected a multitude of New Offices, and sent hither swarms of Officers to harass our people, and eat out their substance.

He has kept among us, in times of peace, Standing Armies without the Consent of our legislature.

He has affected to render the Military independent of and superior to the Civil power.

He has combined with others to subject us to a jurisdiction foreign to our constitution, and unacknowledged by our loss giving his Assent to their Acts of pretended Legislation:

For quartering large bodies of armed troops among us:

For protecting them, by a mock Trial, from punishment for any Murders which they should commit on the Inhabitants of these States:

For cutting off our Trade with all parts of the world:

For imposing Taxes on us without our Consent:

For depriving us in many cases of the benefits of Trial by jury:

For transporting us beyond Seas to be tried for pretended

offences:

For abolishing the free System of English Laws in a neighboring Province, establishing therein an Arbitrary government, and enlarging its Boundaries so as to render it at once an example and fit instrument for introducing the same absolute rule into these Colonies:

For taking away our Charters, abolishing our most valuable Laws, and altering fundamentally the Forms of our Governments:

For suspending our own Legislatures, and declaring themselves invested with power to legislate for us in all cases whatsoever.

He has abdicated Government here, by declaring us out of his Protection and waging war against us.

He has plundered our seas, ravaged our Coasts, burnt our towns, and destroyed the lives of our people.

He is at this time transporting large Armies of foreign Mercenaries to complete the works of death, desolation and tyranny, already begun with circumstances of Cruelty and perfidy scarcely paralleled in the most barbarous ages, and totally unworthy the Head of a civilized nation.

He has constrained our fellow Citizens taken captive on the high Seas to bear Arms against their Country, to become the executioners of their friends and Brethren, or to fall themselves by their Hands.

He has excited domestic insurrections amongst us, and has endeavored to bring on the inhabitants of our frontiers, the merciless Indian Savages, whose known rule of warfare is an undistinguished destruction of all ages, sexes and conditions.

In every stage of these Oppressions We have Petitioned for Redress in the most humble terms. Our repeated Petitions have been answered only by repeated injury. A Prince, whose character is thus Marked by every act which may define a Tyrant, is unfit to be the ruler of a free people.

Nor have We been wanting in attentions to our British brethren. We have warned them from time to time of attempts by their legislature to extend an unwarrantable jurisdiction over us. We have reminded them of the circumstances of our emigration and settlement here. We have appealed to their native justice and magnanimity, and we have conjured them by the ties of our common kindred to disavow these usurpations, which would inevitably interrupt our connections and correspondence. They too have been deaf to the voice of justice and of consanguinity. We must therefore, acquiesce in the necessity which denounces our Separation, and hold them, as we hold the rest of mankind, Enemies in War, in Peace Friends.

WE, THEREFORE, the REPRESENTATIVES of the UNITED STATES OF AMERICA, IN GENERAL CONGRESS, Assembled, appealing to the *Supreme Judge of the world* for the rectitude of our intentions, do, in the Name, and by the authority of the good People of these Colonies, solemnly PUBLISH and DECLARE, That these United Colonies are, and of Right ought to be FREE AND INDEPENDENT States; that they are Absolved from all Allegiance to the British Crown, and that all political connection between them and the State of Great Britain, is and ought to be totally dissolved; and that as FREE AND INDEPENDENT STATES, they have full Power to levy War, conclude Peace, contract Alliances, establish Commerce, and to do all other Acts and Things which INDEPENDENT STATES may of right do. And for the support of this Declaration, with a firm reliance on the protection of *Divine Providence,* We mutually pledge to each other our Lives, our Fortunes, and our sacred Honor.

APPENDIX C

The Constitution of the United States of America

We the People of the United States, in Order to form a more perfect Union, establish Justice, insure domestic Tranquility, provide for the common defence, promote the general Welfare, and secure the Blessings of Liberty to ourselves and our Posterity, do ordain and establish this Constitution for the United States of America.

ARTICLE I.

SECTION 1. All legislative Powers herein granted shall be vested in a Congress of the United States, which shall consist of a Senate and House of Representatives.

SECTION 2. The House of Representatives shall be composed of Members chosen every second Year by the People of the several States, and the Electors in each State shall have the Qualifications requisite for Electors of the most numerous Branch of the State Legislature.

No Person shall be a Representative who shall not have attained to the Age of twenty-five Years, and been seven Years a Citizen of the United States, and who shall not, when elected, be an Inhabitant of that State in which he shall be chosen.

[Representatives and direct Taxes shall be apportioned among the several States which may be included within this Union,

---

[NOTE: This booklet presents the Constitution and all amendments in their original form. Items which have since been amended or superseded, as identified in the footnotes, are bracketed.]

according to their respective Numbers, which shall be determined by adding to the whole Number of free Persons, including those bound to Service for a Term of Years, and excluding Indians not taxed, three fifths of all other Persons.]* The actual Enumeration shall be made within three Years after the first Meeting of the Congress of the United States, and within every subsequent Term of ten Years, in such Manner as they shall by Law direct. The Number of Representatives shall not exceed one for every thirty Thousand,** but each State shall have at Least one Representative; and until such enumeration shall be made, the State of New Hampshire shall be entitled to chuse three, Massachusetts eight, Rhode-Island and Providence Plantations one, Connecticut five, New-York six, New Jersey four, Pennsylvania eight, Delaware one, Maryland six, Virginia ten, North Carolina five, South Carolina five, and Georgia three.

When vacancies happen in the Representation from any State, the Executive Authority thereof shall issue Writs of Election to fill such Vacancies.

The House of Representatives shall chuse their Speaker and other Officers; and shall have the sole Power of Impeachment.

SECTION 3. The Senate of the United States shall be composed of two Senators from each State, [chosen by the Legislature thereof,]*** for six Years; and each Senator shall have one Vote.

Immediately after they shall be assembled in Consequence of the first Election, they shall be divided as equally as may be into three Classes. The Seats of the Senators of the first Class shall be vacated at the Expiration of the second Year, of the second Class at the Expiration of the fourth Year, and of the third Class at the

---

*Changed by section 2 of the fourteenth amendment.
**Ratio in 1965 was one to over 410,000.
***Changed by section 1 of the seventeenth amendment.

Expiration of the sixth Year, so that one-third may be chosen every second Year; [and if Vacancies happen by Resignation, or otherwise, during the Recess of the Legislature of any State, the Executive thereof may make temporary Appointments until the next Meeting of the Legislature, which shall then fill such Vacancies.]*

No Person shall be a Senator who shall not have attained to the Age of thirty Years, and been nine Years a Citizen of the United States, and who shall not, when elected, be an Inhabitant of that State for which he shall be chosen.

The Vice President of the United States shall be President of the Senate, but shall have no Vote, unless they be equally divided.

The Senate shall chuse their other Officers, and also a President pro tempore, in the absence of the Vice President, or when he shall exercise the Office of President of the United States.

The Senate shall have the sole Power to try all Impeachments. When sitting for that Purpose, they shall be on Oath or Affirmation. When the President of the United States is tried, the Chief Justice shall preside: And no Person shall be convicted without the Concurrence of two thirds of the Members present.

Judgment in Cases of Impeachment shall not extend further than to removal from Office, and disqualification to hold and enjoy any Office of honor, Trust or Profit under the United States: but the Party convicted shall nevertheless be liable and subject to Indictment, Trial, Judgment and Punishment, according to Law.

SECTION 4. The Times, Places and Manner of holding Elections for Senators and Representatives, shall be prescribed in each State by the Legislature thereof; but the Congress may at any time by Law make or alter such Regulations, except as to the Place of Chusing Senators.

---

*Changed by clause 2 of the seventeenth amendment.

The Congress shall assemble at least once in every Year, and such Meeting shall [be on the first Monday in December,]** unless they shall by Law appoint a different Day.

SECTION 5. Each House shall be the Judge of the Elections, Returns and Qualifications of its own Members, and a Majority of each shall constitute a Quorum to do Business; but a smaller number may adjourn from day to day, and may be authorized to compel the Attendance of absent Members, in such Manner, and under such Penalties as each House may provide.

Each House may determine the Rules of its Proceedings, punish its Members for disorderly Behavior, and, with the Concurrence of two thirds, expel a Member.

Each House shall keep a Journal of its Proceedings, and from time to time publish the same, excepting such Parts as may in their Judgment require Secrecy; and the Yeas and Nays of the Members of either House on any question shall, at the Desire of one fifth of those Present, be entered on the Journal.

Neither House, during the Session of Congress, shall, without the Consent of the other, adjourn for more than three days, nor to any other Place than that in which the two Houses shall be sitting.

SECTION 6. The Senators and Representatives shall receive a Compensation for their Services, to be ascertained by Law, and paid out of the Treasury of the United States. They shall in all Cases, except Treason, Felony and Breach of the Peace, be privileged from Arrest during their Attendance at the Session of their respective Houses, and in going to and returning from the same; and for any Speech or Debate in either House, they shall not be questioned in any other Place.

No Senator or Representative shall, during the Time for which he was elected, be appointed to any civil Office under the Authority of the United States, which shall have been created, or the

---

**Changed by section 2 of the twentieth amendment.

Emoluments whereof shall have been encreased during such time; and no Person holding any Office under the United States, shall be a Member of either House during his Continuance in Office.

Section 7. All Bills for raising Revenue shall originate in the House of Representatives; but the Senate may propose or concur with Amendments as on other Bills.

Every Bill which shall have passed the House of Representatives and the Senate, shall, before it become a Law, be presented to the President of the United States; If he approve he shall sign it, but if not he shall return it, with his Objections to that House in which it shall have originated, who shall enter the Objections at large on their Journal, and proceed to reconsider it. If after such Reconsideration two thirds of that House shall agree to pass the Bill, it shall be sent, together with the Objections, to the other House, by which it shall likewise be reconsidered, and if approved by two thirds of that House, it shall become a Law. But in all such Cases the Votes of both Houses shall be determined by Yeas and Nays, and the Names of the Persons voting for and against the Bill shall be entered on the Journal of each House respectively. If any Bill shall not be returned by the President within ten Days (Sundays excepted) after it shall have been presented to him, the Same shall be a Law, in like Manner as if he had signed it, unless the Congress by their Adjournment prevent its Return, in which Case it shall not be a Law.

Every Order, Resolution, or Vote to which the Concurrence of the Senate and House of Representatives may be necessary (except on a question of Adjournment) shall be presented to the President of the United States; and before the Same shall take Effect, shall be approved by him, or being disapproved by him, shall be repassed by two thirds of the Senate and House of Representatives, according to the Rules and Limitations prescribed in the Case of a Bill.

SECTION 8. The Congress shall have Power To lay and collect Taxes, Duties, Imposts and Excises, to pay the Debts and provide for the common Defence and general Welfare of the United States; but all Duties, Imposts and Excises shall be uniform throughout the United States;

To borrow money on the credit of the United States;

To regulate Commerce with foreign Nations, and among the several States, and with the Indian Tribes;

To establish an uniform Rule of Naturalization, and uniform Laws on the subject of Bankruptcies throughout the United States;

To coin Money, regulate the Value thereof, and of foreign Coin, and fix the Standard of Weights and Measures;

To provide for the Punishment of counterfeiting the Securities and current Coin of the United States;

To establish Post Offices and post Roads;

To promote the Progress of Science and useful Arts, by securing for limited Times to Authors and Inventors the exclusive Right to their respective Writings and Discoveries;

To constitute Tribunals inferior to the supreme Court;

To define and punish Piracies and Felonies committed on the high Seas, and Offenses against the Law of Nations;

To declare War, grant Letters of Marque and Reprisal, and make Rules concerning Captures on Land and Water;

To raise and support Armies, but no Appropriation of Money to that Use shall be for a longer Term than two Years;

To provide and maintain a Navy;

To make Rules for the Government and Regulation of the land and naval Forces;

To provide for calling forth the Militia to execute the Laws of the Union, suppress Insurrections and repel Invasions;

To provide for organizing, arming, and disciplining the Militia, and for governing such Part of them as may be employed in the Service of the United States, reserving to the States respectively, the Appointment of the Officers, and the Authority of training the Militia according to the discipline prescribed by Congress;

To exercise exclusive Legislation in all Cases whatsoever, over such District (not exceeding ten Miles square) as may, by Cession of particular States, and the acceptance of Congress, become the Seat of the Government of the United States, and to exercise like Authority over all Places purchased by the Consent of the Legislature of the State in which the Same shall be, for the Erection of Forts, Magazines, Arsenals, dock-Yards, and other needful Buildings;—And

To make all Laws which shall be necessary and proper for carrying into Execution the foregoing Powers, and all other Powers vested by this Constitution in the Government of the United States, or in any Department or Officer thereof.

SECTION 9. The Migration or Importation of such Persons as any of the States now existing shall think proper to admit, shall not be prohibited by the Congress prior to the Year one thousand eight hundred and eight, but a tax or duty may be imposed on such Importation, not exceeding ten dollars for each Person.

The privilege of the Writ of Habeas Corpus shall not be suspended, unless when in Cases of Rebellion or Invasion the public Safety may require it.

No Bill of Attainder or ex post facto Law shall be passed.

No capitation, or other direct, Tax shall be laid, unless in Proportion to the Census or Enumeration herein before directed to be taken.*

No Tax or Duty shall be laid on Articles exported from any State.

---

* But see the sixteenth amendment.

No Preference shall be given by any Regulation of Commerce or Revenue to the Ports of one State over those of another: nor shall Vessels bound to, or from, one State, be obliged to enter, clear, or pay Duties in another.

No Money shall be drawn from the Treasury, but in Consequence of Appropriations made by Law; and a regular Statement and Account of the Receipts and Expenditures of all public Money shall be published from time to time.

No Title of Nobility shall be granted by the United States: And no Person holding any Office of Profit or Trust under them, shall, without the Consent of the Congress, accept of any present, Emolument, Office, or Title, of any kind whatever, from any King, Prince, or foreign State.

SECTION 10. No State shall enter into any Treaty, Alliance, or Confederation; grant Letters of Marque and Reprisal; coin Money; emit Bills of Credit; make any Thing but gold and silver Coin a Tender in Payment of Debts; pass any Bill of Attainder, ex post facto Law, or Law impairing the Obligation of Contracts, or grant any Title of Nobility.

No State shall, without the Consent of the Congress, lay any Imposts or Duties on Imports or Exports, except what may be absolutely necessary for executing its inspection Laws: and the net Produce of all Duties and Imposts, laid by any State on Imports or Exports, shall be for the Use of the Treasury of the United States; and all such Laws shall be subject to the Revision and Controul of the Congress.

No State shall, without the Consent of Congress, lay any duty of Tonnage, keep Troops, or Ships of War in time of Peace, enter into any Agreement or Compact with another State, or with a foreign Power, or engage in War, unless actually invaded, or in such imminent Danger as will not admit of delay.

ARTICLE II.

SECTION 1. The executive Power shall be vested in a **President** of the United States of America. He shall hold his Office during the Term of four Years, and, together with the Vice-President, chosen for the same Term, be elected, as follows.

Each State shall appoint, in such Manner as the Legislature thereof may direct, a Number of Electors, equal to the whole Number of Senators and Representatives to which the State may be entitled in the Congress: but no Senator or Representative, or Person holding an Office of Trust or Profit under the United States, shall be appointed an Elector.

[The Electors shall meet in their respective States, and vote by Ballot for two persons, of whom one at least shall not be an Inhabitant of the same State with themselves. And they shall make a List of all the Persons voted for, and of the Number of Votes for each; which List they shall sign and certify, and transmit sealed to the Seat of the Government of the United States, directed to the President of the Senate. The President of the Senate shall, in the Presence of the Senate and House of Representatives, open all the Certificates, and the Votes shall then be counted. The Person having the greatest Number of Votes shall be the President, if such Number be a Majority of the whole Number of Electors appointed; and if there be more than one who have such Majority, and have an equal Number of Votes, then the House of Representatives shall immediately chuse by Ballot one of them for President; and if no Person have a Majority, then from the five highest on the List the said House shall in like Manner chuse the President. But in chusing the President, the Votes shall be taken by **States**, the Representation from each State having one Vote; a quorum for this Purpose shall consist of a Member or Members from **two** thirds of the States, and a Majority of all the States shall be necessary to a Choice. In every Case, after the Choice of the **President,** the Person having the greatest Number of Votes of the Electors shall be the Vice President. But if there should remain two or more who have equal Votes, the Senate shall chuse from them by Ballot the Vice-President.]*

The Congress may determine the Time of chusing the Electors, and the Day on which they shall give their Votes; which Day shall be the same throughout the United States.

No person except a natural born Citizen, or a Citizen of the United States, at the time of the Adoption of this Constitution, shall be eligible to the Office of President; neither shall any Person be eligible to that Office who shall not have attained to the Age of thirty-five Years, and been fourteen Years a Resident within the United States.

**[In Case of the Removal of the President from Office, or of his Death, Resignation, or Inability to discharge the Powers and Duties of the said Office, the same shall devolve on the Vice President, and the Congress may by Law, provide for the Case of Removal, Death, Resignation or Inability, both of the President and Vice President, declaring what Officer shall then act as President, and such Officer shall act accordingly, until the Disability be removed, or a President shall be elected.]

The President shall, at stated Times, receive for his Services, a Compensation, which shall neither be encreased nor diminished during the Period for which he shall have been elected, and he shall not receive within that Period any other Emolument from the United States, or any of them.

Before he enter on the Execution of his Office, he shall take the following Oath or Affirmation:—"I do solemnly swear (or affirm) that I will faithfully execute the Office of President of the United

---

*Superseded by the twelfth amendment.
**This clause has been affected by the twenty-fifth amendment.

States, and will to the best of my Ability, preserve, protect and defend the Constitution of the United States."

SECTION 2. The President shall be Commander in Chief of the Army and Navy of the United States, and of the Militia of the several States, when called into the actual Service of the United States; he may require the Opinion in writing, of the principal Officer in each of the executive Departments, upon any subject relating to the Duties of their respective Offices, and he shall have Power to Grant Reprieves and Pardons for Offenses against the United States, except in Cases of Impeachment.

He shall have Power, by and with the Advice and Consent of the Senate, to make Treaties, provided two-thirds of the Senators present concur; and he shall nominate, and by and with the Advice and Consent of the Senate, shall appoint Ambassadors, other public Ministers and Consuls, Judges of the supreme Court, and all other Officers of the United States, whose Appointments are not herein otherwise provided for, and which shall be established by Law: but the Congress may by Law vest the Appointment of such inferior Officers, as they think proper, in the President alone, in the Courts of Law, or in the Heads of Departments.

The President shall have Power to fill up all Vacancies that may happen during the Recess of the Senate, by granting Commissions which shall expire at the End of their next Session.

SECTION 3. He shall from time to time give to the Congress Information of the State of the Union, and recommend to their Consideration such Measures as he shall judge necessary and expedient; he may, on extraordinary Occasions, convene both Houses, or either of them, and in Case of Disagreement between them, with Respect to the Time of Adjournment, he may adjourn them to such Time as he shall think proper; he shall receive Ambassadors and other public Ministers; he shall take Care that the Laws be faithfully executed, and shall Commission all the Officers of the United States.

SECTION 4. The President, Vice President and all civil Officers of the United States, shall be removed from Office on Impeachment for, and Conviction of, Treason, Bribery, or other high Crimes and Misdemeanors.

ARTICLE III.

SECTION 1. The judicial Power of the United States, shall be vested in one supreme Court, and in such inferior Courts as the Congress may from time to time ordain and establish. The Judges, both of the supreme and inferior Courts, shall hold their Offices during good Behaviour, and shall, at stated Times, receive for their Services, a Compensation, which shall not be diminished during their Continuance in Office.

SECTION 2. The judicial Power shall extend to all Cases, in Law and Equity, arising under this Constitution, the Laws of the United States, and Treaties made, or which shall be made, under their Authority;—to all Cases affecting Ambassadors, other public Ministers and Consuls;—to all Cases of admiralty and maritime Jurisdiction;—to Controversies to which the United States shall be a Party;—to Controversies between two or more States;—between a State and Citizens of another State;—between Citizens of different States;—between Citizens of the same State claiming Lands under Grants of different States, and between a State, or the Citizens thereof, and foreign States, Citizens or Subjects.

In all Cases affecting Ambassadors, other public Ministers and Consuls, and those in which a State shall be Party, the supreme Court shall have original Jurisdiction. In all the other Cases before mentioned, the supreme Court shall have appellate Jurisdiction, both as to Law and Fact, with such Exceptions, and under such Regulations as the Congress shall make.

The trial of all Crimes, except in Cases of Impeachment, shall be by Jury; and such Trial shall be held in the State where the said Crimes shall have been committed; but when not committed within any State, the Trial shall be at such Place or Places as the Congress may by Law have directed.

SECTION 3. Treason against the United States, shall consist only in levying War against them, or in adhering to their Enemies, giving them Aid and Comfort. No Person shall be convicted of Treason unless on the Testimony of two Witnesses to the same overt Act, or on Confession in open Court.

The Congress shall have Power to declare the Punishment of Treason, but no Attainder of Treason shall work Corruption of Blood, or Forfeiture except during the Life of the Person attainted.

ARTICLE IV.

SECTION 1. Full Faith and Credit shall be given in each State to the public Acts, Records, and judicial Proceedings of every other State. And the Congress may by general Laws prescribe the Manner in which such Acts, Records and Proceedings shall be proved, and the Effect thereof.

SECTION 2. The Citizens of each State shall be entitled to all Privileges and Immunities of Citizens in the several States.

A Person charged in any State with Treason, Felony, or other Crime, who shall flee from Justice, and be found in another State, shall on demand of the executive Authority of the State from which he fled, be delivered up, to be removed to the State having Jurisdiction of the Crime.

[No Person held to Service or Labour in one State, under the Laws thereof, escaping into another, shall, in Consequence of any Law or Regulation therein, be discharged from such Service or

Labour, but shall be delivered up on Claim of the Party to whom such Service or Labour may be due.]*

SECTION 3. New States may be admitted by the Congress into this Union; but no new State shall be formed or erected within the Jurisdiction of any other State; nor any State be formed by the Junction of two or more States, or parts of States, without the Consent of the Legislatures of the States concerned as well as of the Congress.

The Congress shall have Power to dispose of and make all needful Rules and Regulations respecting the Territory or other Property belonging to the United States; and nothing in this Constitution shall be so construed as to Prejudice any Claims of the United States, or of any particular State.

SECTION 4. The United States shall guarantee to every State in this Union a Republican Form of Government, and shall protect each of them against Invasion; and on Application of the Legislature, or of the Executive (when the Legislature cannot be convened) against domestic Violence.

ARTICLE V.

The Congress, whenever two-thirds of both Houses shall deem it necessary, shall propose Amendments to this Constitution, or, on the Application of the Legislatures of two-thirds of the several States, shall call a Convention for proposing Amendments, which, in either Case, shall be valid to all Intents and Purposes, as part of this Constitution, when ratified by the Legislatures of three-fourths of the several States, or by Conventions in three-fourths thereof, as the one or the other Mode of Ratification may be proposed by the Congress: Provided that no Amendment which may be made prior to the Year One thousand eight hundred and eight shall in any Manner affect the first and fourth Clauses in the

---

*Superseded by the thirteenth amendment.

Ninth Section of the first Article; and that no State, without its Consent, shall be deprived of its equal Suffrage in the Senate.

ARTICLE VI.

All Debts contracted and Engagements entered into, before the Adoption of this Constitution, shall be as valid against the United States under this Constitution, as under the Confederation.

This Constitution, and the Laws of the United States which shall be made in Pursuance thereof; and all Treaties made, or which shall be made, under the Authority of the United States, shall be the supreme Law of the Land; and the Judges in every State shall be bound thereby, any Thing in the Constitution or Laws of any State to the Contrary notwithstanding.

The Senators and Representatives before mentioned, and the Members of the several State Legislatures, and all executive and judicial Officers, both of the United States and of the several States, shall be bound by Oath or Affirmation, to support this Constitution; but no religious Test shall ever be required as a Qualification to any Office or public Trust under the United States.

ARTICLE VII.

The Ratification of the Conventions of nine States shall be sufficient for the Establishment of this Constitution between the States so ratifying the Same.

DONE in Convention by the Unanimous Consent of the States present the Seventeenth Day of September in the Year of our Lord one thousand seven hundred and Eighty seven and of the Independence of the United States of America the Twelfth.

In Witness whereof We have hereunto subscribed our Names.

Go *WASHINGTON*
Presidt and deputy from Virginia

New Hampshire.

JOHN LANGDON
NICHOLAS GILMAN

Massachusetts.

NATHANIEL GORHAM
RUFUS KING

New Jersey.

WIL: LIVINGSTON
DAVID BREARLEY.
WM PATERSON.
JONA: DAYTON

Pennsylvania.

B FRANKLIN
ROBT. MORRIS
THOS. FITZSIMONS
JAMES WILSON
THOMAS MIFFLIN
GEO. CLYMER
JARED INGERSOLL
GOUV MORRIS

Delaware.

GEO: READ
JOHN DICKINSON
JACO: BROOM
GUNNING BEDFORD jun
RICHARD BASSETT

Connecticut.

WM SAML JOHNSON
ROGER SHERMAN

New York.

ALEXANDER HAMILTON

Maryland.

JAMES MCHENRY
DANL CARROL
DAN: of ST THOS JENIFER

Virginia.

JOHN BLAIR
JAMES MADISON Jr.

North Carolina.

WM BLOUNT
HU WILLIAMSON
RICHD DOBBS SPAIGHT.

South Carolina.

J. RUTLEDGE
CHARLES PINCKNEY
CHARLES COTESWORTH
    PINCKNEY
PIERCE BUTLER

Georgia.

WILLIAM FEW
ABR BALDWIN

Attest:

WILLIAM JACKSON, *Secretary.*

ARTICLES IN ADDITION TO, AND AMENDMENT OF, THE CONSTITUTION OF THE UNITED STATES OF AMERICA, PROPOSED BY CONGRESS, AND RATIFIED BY THE LEGISLATURES OF THE SEVERAL STATES, PURSUANT TO THE FIFTH ARTICLE OF THE ORIGINAL CONSTITUTION.*

(The first 10 Amendments were ratified December 15, 1791, and form what is known as the "Bill of Rights")

AMENDMENT I

Congress shall make no law respecting an establishment of religion, or prohibiting the free exercise thereof; or abridging the freedom of speech, or of the press; or the right of the people peaceably to assemble, and to petition the Government for a redress of grievances.

AMENDMENT II

A well regulated Militia, being necessary to the security of a free State, the right of the people to keep and bear Arms, shall not be infringed.

AMENDMENT III

No Soldier shall, in time of peace be quartered in any house, without the consent of the Owner, nor in time of war, but in a manner to be prescribed by law.

---

*Amendment XXI was not ratified by state legislatures, but by state conventions summoned by Congress.

AMENDMENT IV

The right of the people to be secure in their persons, houses, papers, and effects, against unreasonable searches and seizures, shall not be violated, and no Warrants shall issue, but upon probable cause, supported by Oath or affirmation, and particularly describing the place to be searched, and the persons or things to be seized.

AMENDMENT V

No person shall be held to answer for a capital, or otherwise infamous crime, unless on a presentment or indictment of a Grand Jury, except in cases arising in the land or naval forces, or in the Militia, when in actual service in time of War or public danger; nor shall any person be subject for the same offence to be twice put in jeopardy of life or limb; nor shall be compelled in any criminal case to be a witness against himself, nor be deprived of life, liberty, or property, without due process of law; nor shall private property be taken for public use, without just compensation.

AMENDMENT VI

In all criminal prosecutions, the accused shall enjoy the right to a speedy and public trial, by an impartial jury of the State and district wherein the crime shall have been committed, which district shall have been previously ascertained by law, and to be informed of the nature and cause of the accusation; to be confronted with the witnesses against him; to have compulsory process for obtaining witnesses in his favor, and to have the Assistance of Counsel for his defence.

AMENDMENT VII

In suits at common law, where the value in controversy shall exceed twenty dollars, the right of trial by jury shall be preserved, and no fact tried by a jury, shall be otherwise reexamined in any

Court of the United States, than according to the rules of the common law.

AMENDMENT VIII

Excessive bail shall not be required, nor excessive fines imposed, nor cruel and unusual punishments inflicted.

AMENDMENT IX

The enumeration in the Constitution, of certain rights, shall not be construed to deny or disparage others retained by the people.

AMENDMENT X

The powers not delegated to the United States by the Constitution, nor prohibited by it to the States, are reserved to the States respectively, or to the people.

AMENDMENT XI

(Ratified February 7, 1795)

The Judicial power of the United States shall not be construed to extend to any suit in law or equity, commenced or prosecuted against one of the United States by Citizens of another State, or by Citizens or Subjects of any Foreign State.

AMENDMENT XII

(Ratified July 27, 1804)

The Electors shall meet in their respective states and vote by ballot for President and Vice-President, one of whom, at least, shall not be an inhabitant of the same state with themselves; they shall name in their ballots the person voted for as President, and in distinct ballots the person voted for as Vice-President, and they shall make distinct lists of all persons voted for as President, and of all persons voted for as Vice-President, and of the number of votes for each, which lists they shall sign and certify, and transmit sealed to the seat of the government of the United States, directed to the President of the Senate;—The President of the Senate shall, in presence of the Senate and House of Representatives, open all the certificates and the votes shall then be counted;— The person having the greatest number of votes for President, shall be the President, if such number be a majority of the whole number of Electors appointed; and if no person have such majority, then from the persons having the highest numbers not exceeding three on the list of those voted for as President, the House of Representatives shall choose immediately, by ballot, the President. But in choosing the President, the votes shall be taken by states, the representation from each state having one vote; a quorum for this purpose shall consist of a member or members from two-thirds of the states, and a majority of all the states shall be necessary to a choice. [And if the House of Representatives shall not choose a President whenever the right of choice shall devolve upon them, before the fourth day of March next following, then the Vice-President shall act as President, as in the case of the death or other constitutional disability of the President.—]* The person having the greatest number of votes as Vice-President, shall be the Vice-President, if such number be a majority of the whole number of Electors appointed, and if no person have a majority, then from the two highest numbers on the list, the Senate shall choose the Vice-President; a quorum for the purpose shall consist of two-thirds of the whole number of Senators, and a majority of the whole number shall be necessary to a choice. But no person constitutionally ineligible to the office of President shall be eligible to that of Vice-President of the United States.

---

*Superseded by section 3 of the twentieth amendment.

AMENDMENT XIII

(Ratified December 6, 1865)

SECTION 1. Neither slavery nor involuntary servitude, except as a punishment for crime whereof the party shall have been duly convicted, shall exist within the United States, or any place subject to their jurisdiction.

SECTION 2. Congress shall have power to enforce this article by appropriate legislation.

AMENDMENT XIV

(Ratified July 9, 1868)

SECTION 1. All persons born or naturalized in the United States, and subject to the jurisdiction thereof, are citizens of the United States and of the State wherein they reside. No State shall make or enforce any law which shall abridge the privileges or immunities of citizens of the United States; nor shall any State deprive any person of life, liberty, or property, without due process of law; nor deny to any person within its jurisdiction the equal protection of the laws.

SECTION 2. Representatives shall be apportioned among the several States according to their respective numbers, counting the whole number of persons in each State, excluding Indians not taxed. But when the right to vote at any election for the choice of electors for President and Vice-President of the United States, Representatives in Congress, the Executive and Judicial officers of a State, or the members of the Legislature thereof, is denied to any of the male inhabitants of such State, being twenty-one years of age,* and citizens of the United States, or in any way abridged, except for participation in rebellion, or other crime, the basis of

---

*Changed by section 1 of the twenty-sixth amendment.

representation therein shall be reduced in the proportion which the number of such male citizens shall bear to the whole number of male citizens twenty-one years of age in such State.

SECTION 3. No person shall be a Senator or Representative in Congress, or elector of President and Vice-President, or hold any office, civil or military, under the United States, or under any State, who, having previously taken an oath, as a member of Congress, or as an officer of the United States, or as a member of any State legislature, or as an executive or judicial officer of any State, to support the Constitution of the United States, shall have engaged in insurrection or rebellion against the same, or given aid or comfort to the enemies thereof. But Congress may by a vote of two-thirds of each House, remove such disability.

SECTION 4. The validity of the public debt of the United States, authorized by law, including debts incurred for payment of pensions and bounties for services in suppressing insurrection or rebellion, shall not be questioned. But neither the United States nor any State shall assume or pay any debt or obligation incurred in aid of insurrection or rebellion against the United States, or any claim for the loss or emancipation of any slave; but all such debts, obligations and claims shall be held illegal and void.

SECTION 5. The Congress shall have power to enforce, by appropriate legislation, the provisions of this article.

AMENDMENT XV

(Ratified February 3, 1870)

SECTION 1. The right of citizens of the United States to vote shall not be denied or abridged by the United States or by any State on account of race, color, or previous condition of servitude—

SECTION 2. The Congress shall have power to enforce this article by appropriate legislation.

AMENDMENT XVI
(Ratified February 3, 1913)

The Congress shall have power to lay and collect taxes on incomes, from whatever source derived, without apportionment among the several States, and without regard to any census or enumeration.

AMENDMENT XVII
(Ratified April 8, 1913)

The Senate of the United States shall be composed of two Senators from each State, elected by the people thereof, for six years; and each Senator shall have one vote. The electors in each State shall have the qualifications requisite for electors of the most numerous branch of the State legislatures.

When vacancies happen in the representation of any State in the Senate, the executive authority of such State shall issue writs of election to fill such vacancies: *Provided,* That the legislature of any State may empower the executive thereof to make temporary appointments until the people fill the vacancies by election as the legislature may direct.

This amendment shall not be so construed as to affect the election or term of any Senator chosen before it becomes valid as part of the Constitution.

AMENDMENT XVIII
(Ratified January 16, 1919)

[SECTION 1. After one year from the ratification of this article the manufacture, sale, or transportation of intoxicating liquors within, the importation thereof into, or the exportation thereof from the United States and all territory subject to the jurisdiction thereof for beverage purposes is hereby prohibited.

[SECTION 2. The Congress and the several States shall have concurrent power to enforce this article by appropriate legislation.

[SECTION 3. This article shall be inoperative unless it shall have been ratified as an amendment to the Constitution by the legislatures of the several States as provided in the Constitution, within seven years from the date of the submission hereof to the States by the Congress.]*

AMENDMENT XIX
(Ratified August 18, 1920)

The right of citizens of the United States to vote shall not be denied or abridged by the United States or by any State on account of sex.

Congress shall have power to enforce this article by appropriate legislation.

AMENDMENT XX
(Ratified January 23, 1933)

SECTION 1. The terms of the President and Vice President shall end at noon on the 20th day of January, and the terms of Senators and Representatives at noon on the 3d day of January, of the years in which such terms would have ended if this article had not been ratified; and the terms of their successors shall then begin.

SECTION 2. The Congress shall assemble at least once in every year, and such meeting shall begin at noon on the 3d day of January, unless they shall by law appoint a different day.

SECTION 3. If, at the time fixed for the beginning of the term of the President, the President elect shall have died, the Vice President elect shall become President. If a President shall not have been chosen before the time fixed for the beginning of his term, or if the President elect shall have failed to qualify, then the Vice President elect shall act as President until a President shall have qualified; and the Congress may by law provide for the case

---
*Repealed by section 1 of the twenty-first amendment.

wherein neither a President elect nor a Vice President elect shall have qualified, declaring who shall then act as President, or the manner in which one who is to act shall be selected, and such person shall act accordingly until a President or Vice President shall have qualified.

SECTION 4. The Congress may by law provide for the case of the death of any of the persons from whom the House of Representatives may choose a President whenever the right of choice shall have devolved upon them, and for the case of the death of any of the persons from whom the Senate may choose a Vice President whenever the right of choice shall have devolved upon them.

SECTION 5. Sections 1 and 2 shall take effect on the 15th day of October following the ratification of this article.

SECTION 6. This article shall be inoperative unless it shall have been ratified as an amendment to the Constitution by the legislatures of three-fourths of the several States within seven years from the date of its submission.

AMENDMENT XXI

(Ratified December 5, 1933)

SECTION 1. The eighteenth article of amendment to the Constitution of the United States is hereby repealed.

SECTION 2. The transportation or importation into any State, Territory, or possession of the United States for delivery or use therein of intoxicating liquors, in violation of the laws thereof, is hereby prohibited.

SECTION 3. This article shall be inoperative unless it shall have been ratified as an amendment to the Constitution by conventions in the several States, as provided in the Constitution, within seven years from the date of the submission hereof to the States by the Congress.

AMENDMENT XXII
(Ratified February 27, 1951)

SECTION 1. No person shall be elected to the office of the President more than twice, and no person who has held the office of President, or acted as President, for more than two years of a term to which some other person was elected President shall be elected to the office of the President more than once. But this Article shall not apply to any person holding the office of President when this Article was proposed by the Congress, and shall not prevent any person who may be holding the office of President, or acting as President, during the term within which this Article becomes operative from holding the office of President or acting as President during the remainder of such term.

SECTION 2. This article shall be inoperative unless it shall have been ratified as an amendment to the Constitution by the legislatures of three-fourths of the several States within seven years from the date of its submission to the States by the Congress.

AMENDMENT XXIII
(Ratified March 29, 1961)

SECTION 1. The District constituting the seat of Government of the United States shall appoint in such manner as the Congress may direct:

A number of electors of President and Vice President equal to the whole number of Senators and Representatives in Congress to which the District would be entitled if it were a State, but in no event more than the least populous State; they shall be in addition to those appointed by the States, but they shall be considered, for the purposes of the election of President and Vice President, to be electors appointed by a State; and they shall meet in the District and perform such duties as provided by the twelfth article of amendment.

SECTION 2. The Congress shall have power to enforce this article by appropriate legislation.

AMENDMENT XXIV
(Ratified January 23, 1964)

SECTION 1. The right of citizens of the United States to vote in any primary or other election for President or Vice President, for electors for President or Vice President, or for Senator or Representative in Congress, shall not be denied or abridged by the United States or any State by reason of failure to pay any poll tax or other tax.

SECTION 2. The Congress shall have power to enforce this article by appropriate legislation.

AMENDMENT XXV
(Ratified February 10, 1967)

SECTION 1. In case of the removal of the President from office or of his death or resignation, the Vice President shall become President.

SECTION 2. Whenever there is a vacancy in the office of the Vice President, the President shall nominate a Vice President who shall take office upon confirmation by a majority vote of both Houses of Congress.

SECTION 3. Whenever the President transmits to the President pro tempore of the Senate and the Speaker of the House of Representatives his written declaration that he is unable to discharge the powers and duties of his office, and until he transmits to them a written declaration to the contrary, such powers and duties shall be discharged by the Vice President as Acting President.

SECTION 4. Whenever the Vice President and a majority of either the principal officers of the executive departments or of such other body as Congress may by law provide, transmit to the

President pro tempore of the Senate and the Speaker of the House of Representatives their written declaration that the President is unable to discharge the powers and duties of his office, the Vice President shall immediately assume the powers and duties of the office as Acting President.

Thereafter, when the President transmits to the President pro tempore of the Senate and the Speaker of the House of Representatives his written declaration that no inability exists, he shall resume the powers and duties of his office unless the Vice President and a majority of either the principal officers of the executive department or of such other body as Congress may by law provide, transmit within four days to the President pro tempore of the Senate and the Speaker of the House of Representatives their written declaration that the President is unable to discharge the powers and duties of his office. Thereupon Congress shall decide the issue, assembling within forty-eight hours for that purpose if not in session. If the Congress, within twenty-one days after receipt of the latter written declaration, or, if Congress is not in session, within twenty-one days after Congress is required to assemble, determines by two-thirds vote of both Houses that the President is unable to discharge the powers and duties of his office, the Vice President shall continue to discharge the same as Acting President; otherwise, the President shall resume the powers and duties of his office.

AMENDMENT XXVI

(Ratified July 1, 1971)

SECTION 1. The right of citizens of the United States, who are eighteen years of age or older, to vote shall not be denied or abridged by the United States or by any State on account of age.

SECTION 2. The Congress shall have power to enforce this article by appropriate legislation.

Index

A
Adams, John, 3
American Bar Association, 159
American Medical Association (AMA), 11, 46-47
Anaconda Copper, 85, 94
Anderson, Jack, 18, 45, 106, 148
Anderson-Clayton, 74
André (Grain), 68
Armour, 74-75
Aspen Institute for Humanistic Studies, 21
AT&T, 103, 162
Atlantic Richfield (ARCO), 85

B
Baker, James, 31
Ball, George W., 79
Bank of America, 63
Bank of England, 4
Bergland, Robert, 62, 70-71
Bernhard, Prince, 18-19
Bilderbergers, 18-19, 32-33, 147
Bluestone, Barry, 155
Boggs, Lindy, 89
Boyd, James, 56
British Parliament, Revolutionary War, 4
Broder, David, 27
Brazil, 139
Brooke-Liebig, 74
Brown, Harold, 21
Brzezinski, Zbigniew, 20-21
Budge, Hamer, 49
Bumpers, Dale, 132
Bunge & Born, 68, 74
Bush, George, 30-31
Butz, Earl, 60

C
Carolina Power & Light Company, 100-102
Cargill (Grain), 68, 72, 74
Carnation, 74
Carter, "Jimmy," 20-25, 29, 34, 46, 86, 92
Casey, William, 30
Celanese, 72
Chase-Manhattan Bank, 17, 26, 87, 152
China, 19, 143, 158
Church, Frank, 47-48
Churchill, Winston, 156
Citicorp, 153
Club of Rome, 32, 147
Coca-Cola, 68
Commodity Credit Corporation, 60
Conoco, 56
Consolidated Grain Company, 60
Continental (Grain), 68
Continental Illinois National Bank, 66
Costanzo, G.A., 153
Council on Foreign Relations (CFR), 16-18, 21-22, 30-31, 33-39, 113, 147, 161
CPC, 74
Cuba, 61
Cudahy, 74-75

D
Dahlberg, Kenneth, 73
Davis-Bacon Act, 10
Del Monte, 74
Don Bell Reports, 163-165
Donovan, Raymond, 10
Downey, Thomas J., 48
Duke Power Company, 100-102
Dupont, 56
Dreyfus, Louis (Grain), 68

E
Eisenhower, Dwight, 93
Export-Import Bank, 33
Exxon, 56, 87, 126, 162-163

F
Fair Campaign Practice Act, 11, 43
Federal Reserve Act, 8-9
Fitzgerald, A. Ernest, 106
Ford, Gerald, 31, 48, 94
Ford, Henry, & grandson, 136-137
Ford Foundation, 137
Ford Motor Company, 137, 139
Fort Knox, 8
Franklin, George, 25
F.R.E.E., 34, 36-39

G
General Dynamics, 106
General Motors, 139, 163

247

Genocide Treaty, 158-159
Getty Oil, 57, 67, 85
Grant, Ulysses, 7
Gulf Oil Corporation, 57, 85-86
Guyana, 61

H

Hamilton, Alexander, 6
Hammer, Armand, 75
Hammond, Jay S., 84
Hansen, George, 28
Harrison, Bennett, 155
Hart, Gary, 35
Harvey, Paul, 50, 68, 85, 124, 179-180
Hatch Act, 43
Helms, Jesse, 116, 161
Hewett, Abram S., 129
Hiss, Alger, 157
House, Edward Mandel, 8, 16, 151
Hughes, Howard, 42-43
Hunt, Nelson Bunker, 123

I

International Finance Corporation, 152
International Monetary Fund (IMF), 32-33, 152
Iowa Beef Processors, 75
Iran, 12, 26-29
I.T.T., 72

J

Jackson, Andrew, 7
Jackson, Henry, 19
Japan, 20, 47-48, 77, 88-89, 94, 139-140, 149, 153-156
Jefferson, Thomas, 3, 6
Johnson, Lyndon, 110

K

Kama River Truck Factory, 142
Kennedy, John, 110
King George III, 4, 190
Kirkpatrick, Jean, 160
Kissinger, Henry, 18, 22, 26, 31, 79-80
Knight, John A., 109-110
Korea, 47, 153, 157
Kraft, 74
Kreps, Juanita, 46
Kuhn, Loeb, & Company, 8

L

Langer, William, 157
Law of the Sea Treaty, 158
Leyman, John, 61
Lincoln, Abraham, 7
Lindbergh, Charles A., 41-42
Linowitz, Sol, 24
Long, Russell, 124
Los Angeles Times Mirror Corporation, 67
Lundsburg, Frederick, 170

M

Madison, James, 3
Marathon Oil Company, 57
Martin, James C., 127
Martin, Rose, 160
McArthur, John D., 137
McGreer, G.G., 171-172
McLean Trucking Company, 67
McNamara, Robert S., 22
Merrill, Lynch, Pierce, Fenner & Smith, 66
Metzenbaum, Howard, 132
Mobil Oil, 57, 86, 163-164
Moffett, Tobby, 49
Mondale, Walter, 10, 21, 34-35, 122-123
Monroe, James, 3

N

National Taxpayer's Union, 115-116, 166
Nestles, 74
Nicaragua, 61
Nixon, Richard, 18-19, 31, 60, 93, 110

O

O'Hara, Thomas J., 89-90
OPEC, 79, 81-83

P

Panama Canal, 12, 23-26, 88
Peccei, Aurelio, 32
Percy, Charles, 159, 186
Plant Variety Protection Act, 71, 73
Plymouth Rock Foundation, 160-161
Porter, Sylvia, 125
Proxmire, William, 105-106, 159
Prudential Life Insurance Company, 67
Purex, 72

R

Ralston Purina Food Corporation, 60
Rank, Everett, 70

Reagan, Ronald, 10, 30-34, 89, 93, 119, 126-128, 150, 161-162, 181
Rockefeller, David, 17, 20, 25-26, 31, 79, 87, 157, 163
Rockefeller, Lawrence, 18
Rockefeller, Nelson, 17-18, 123
Roosevelt, Franklin D., 9, 110, 156
Rosenthal (Rep., D-NY), 48
Rothschild, House of, 8
Rusk, Dean, 20

S
Sadat, Anwar, 113
Salassie, Haile, 116-117
SALT II Treaty, 23
Santini, Jim, 18
Schlesinger, James, 107
Schroder, Patricia, 49
Sears, John, 30
Shah of Iran, 26-29, 137
Sheffield, William, 84-85
Simon, William E., 79, 131
Solzhenitsyn, Alexsandr, 142
Sparks, John A., 154-155
Standard Fruit, 74
Standard Oil of California (SOCAL), 57
Stalin, Joseph, 156
Steinbeck, John, 63
Stewart, Johnny (F.R.E.E.), 34, 36-39
Stockman, David, 126-127
Sutton, Anthony, 22
Swift, 74-75

T
Tenneco, 67
Texaco, 57, 85

Thatcher, Margaret, 160
Trible, Paul, 89
Trilateral Commission, 19-26, 30-39, 147, 155

U
Ullman, Al, 124
Unilever, 74
United Nations, 156-161
Union Carbide, 72
United Brands, 74
Upjohn, 72
USSR, 19, 22, 59-61, 75, 90-91, 113, 117, 142-143, 146, 157

V
Vanik, Charles A., 60, 131-132
Vance, Cyrus, 21
Vietnam, 110, 112, 157

W
Walt, Gen. Lewis, 157-158
Warner Communications, 141
Washington, George, 3
Webb, Geoffrey, 95
Weidenbaum, Murray S., 50
Williams, Lindsey, 82-83
Williams, Walter, 190
Wilson (Co.), 74-75
Wilson, Woodrow, 7-8, 109-110, 151
Winn, Larry, 186
World Bank, 152

Quantity prices for *Honest Government:*

5 copies for $25
10 copies for $45
30 copies for $95 (box)

(All postpaid if prepaid.)

If you liked
Honest Government
you'll love these NPL bestsellers!

Honest Money

Eminent surgeon cuts through all the confused thought on this subject and points to economic freedom.
- Tells how to abolish the Fed.
- Gives step-by-step process to an honest monetary system.

An idea whose time has come; a certain hit!
5-3/8 x 8, 200 pp.   **$5**

The Church and the Sword

Captain G. Russell Evans and Dr. C. Gregg Singer counter the "peace movement" with shocking documentation of Red subversion through the National Council of Churches. A powerful Biblical apologetic against pacifism. *2nd Ed.*
5-3/8 x 8, 178 pp. **$5**

The Return of the Puritans

Pat Brooks' classic on Christianity vs. socialism in mortal combat points the way back from degeneracy to divine favor for the U.S. In its 4th great edition, our bestseller is better than ever!
5-3/8 x 8, 208 pp.   **$5**

Send $1 shipping if order is less than $10

New Puritan Library	NC residents add 3% tax	**New Puritan Library**	CA residents add 6% tax
91 Lytle Road Fletcher, NC 28732 (Home Office) (704) 628-2185		P.O. Box 247 Walnut Creek, CA 94596 (Rockies and West) (415) 934-7019	